Acting and Directing Shakespeare's Comedies

Acting and Directing Shakespeare's Comedies: Key Lessons outlines a clear, effective process for acting Shakespeare's comedies.

This book lays out core principles and useful exercises that help the reader better understand, experience, and implement Shakespeare's comedic design. Building off of modern acting methods as well as contemporary Clown, classical Commedia, and verse-speaking techniques, the author guides the reader toward interpretive and performance choices that are original, justified, and entertaining. Included are clear examples and detailed case studies that illuminate and reenforce these key lessons.

This accessible book is for actors, directors, students of Shakespeare, and those who want a fuller, richer awareness of the possibilities within Shakespeare's comedies and a clear, pragmatic process for creating those performances.

Kevin Otos is a professor of theatre at Elon University, North Carolina where he teaches acting, Shakespeare, Commedia, and Clown. He is a professional actor and director, and co-author of *Applied Meisner for the 21st-Century Actor* written with his colleague, Kim Shively.

KEVIN OTOS

Acting and Directing Shakespeare's Comedies
Key Lessons

NEW YORK AND LONDON

Designed cover image: © Kate Conway as Beatrice in Elon University's 2014 *Much Ado about Nothing* directed by Kevin Otos. Costume Design by Jessica Edwards. Photo by Scott Mutherbaugh.

First published 2023
by Routledge
605 Third Avenue, New York, NY 10158

and by Routledge
4 Park Square, Milton Park, Abingdon, Oxon, OX14 4RN

Routledge is an imprint of the Taylor & Francis Group, an informa business

© 2023 Kevin Otos

The right of Kevin Otos to be identified as author of this work has been asserted in accordance with sections 77 and 78 of the Copyright, Designs and Patents Act 1988.

All rights reserved. No part of this book may be reprinted or reproduced or utilized in any form or by any electronic, mechanical, or other means, now known or hereafter invented, including photocopying and recording, or in any information storage or retrieval system, without permission in writing from the publishers.

Trademark notice: Product or corporate names may be trademarks or registered trademarks, and are used only for identification and explanation without intent to infringe.

ISBN: 978-1-032-22743-6 (hbk)
ISBN: 978-1-032-22742-9 (pbk)
ISBN: 978-1-003-27396-7 (ebk)

DOI: 10.4324/9781003273967

Typeset in Joanna MT
by codeMantra

The appendix was originally published in
Applied Meisner for the 21st-Century Actor
by Kevin Otos and Kim Shively (Routledge, 2021).
Reproduced by permission of Taylor & Francis Group.

For Grace and Hannah,

who only laugh when I'm funny.

Contents

Foreword by Sean Boyd viii
Acknowledgements xii

Introduction and Foundations One 1

Under the Commedia Influence Two 13

Misrule and Fools Three 34

Lessons from the Clown World Four 43

Language: Clarity, Variety, and Humor Five 74

Character Studies Six 105

Parting Words Seven 138

Appendix 143
Bibliography 149

Foreword

Kevin and I go back more than two decades now, and I've always known him to have a deep passion for the practice of performing comedy and Shakespeare's plays. There's something more though: his commitment to understanding the potential of the actor's physical life (and in particular, the important role of the breath) in the process of creation. Kevin's dedication to these, and how they coalesce into performance, elevates his teaching from the analytical to the experiential, which serves him well as a teacher and as the author of this book.

Kevin is an artist, a creator (in the modern parlance), and a practitioner. He teaches, he publishes, he professor-ers, but, importantly, he's someone who comes to the craft from the trenches. Someone who hustled. Who stayed mindful and hungry through training, auditions, rehearsals, and in performance. He's also done the research into the history, the texts, and the lineages of practice. More simply . . . Kevin does (and has done) what he asks of any student, director, actor, or contributor. Kevin's an actor who teaches actors, and a director who directs actors. Now, he has written a book for actors, directors, and teachers.

Introducing another text addressing the performance of Shakespeare's plays brings an inherent risk to an author. It has to overcome predilections, loyalties, even siloed tribalism to how Shakespeare needs, should, or must be performed.

What Kevin has created, however, isn't another in a host of tomes anchored in the arithmetic of scansion, meter, and hard arguments about where a "proper" pause can or must come when performing Shakespeare.

Kevin's not interested in barriers, or in writing a treatise on the evolution of meter in English dramatic literature. And . . . thank God. He's interested in bridges, communion, ease, flow, activation, and results. You can't math your way into acting, and certainly not into comedy—and yes, I just used math as a verb. Acting is an embodied, holistic experience. It's a communion between self and other. It's physical—a physicality that shapes action, presence, the body, the breath, the voice, relationship, and story. Kevin gets that.

Every chapter holds excellent insights into how the text informs the characters and the responsibilities the actor and director have to allow the text to inform their process. Kevin does the important work of setting all the lessons, guidance, and exercises into the language of practice and participation, further inviting you to not simply read this book but to use it as a pathway in experimentation and exploration.

Oh, yes, there's some good history in here. In Chapter 2, "Under the Commedia Influence," he lays out Commedia's impact on Shakespeare and how it shaped the expectations of an Elizabethan audience. Kevin connects a lot of the dots for us between Commedia and Shakespeare: how stock characters are represented in the plays, how the stories unfold, and how what the audience had come to expect from a play is serviced by Shakespeare. In Chapter 3, "Misrule and Fools," Kevin details the differences between actors Will Kemp and Robert Armin and how those differences are reflected in the characters they individually performed and how that affected the storytelling.

In Chapter 4, "Lessons from the Clown World," Kevin lays out a process of how to make the most of the opportunity of playing one of Shakespeare's clowns. He blends contemporary examples of the same techniques used from Commedia (and probably before) and details how an actor can use these techniques as a springboard for their own actionable discoveries. This chapter also lifts the conversation on the use of breath beyond the mechanics for supporting the spoken word, toward its importance in communing with the audience and reinforcing character. Chapter 5, "Language: Clarity, Variety, and Humor," dances wonderfully through multiple tools to help artists engage with the texts. By couching everything through the focus of clarity, variety, and humor, Kevin sidesteps the trap of a mechanical attack on the language and keeps the organic quality of this book and his approach to performing these plays.

But it's in Chapter 6, "Character Studies," where Kevin makes his strongest contribution. Using a number of Shakespeare's clowns, Kevin anchors the tools laid out in the previous chapters into an easy-to-follow process using a simple Q&A structure. Through Bottom, Don Armando, Feste, and others, the important lessons in this book are activated, providing a pathway to analysis and practice. My favorite was Don Armando, but I was also excited to see some of the clowns not often given much air in the "clown character rundown," such as Cloten.

This is a book of practice, for practitioners, from a practitioner. It lays out a host of usable tools and strategies meant to be understood through activation—physically investing and executing what you're reading—not just to be ruminated on. And Kevin's done so in a practical way, in small, bite-sized chunks for easy intake and digestion. Tapas, if you will, for the performing of Shakespeare's comedies. He's tethered together the insights of decades of classes, directing and acting gigs, coaching sessions, and insights from innumerable colleagues and mentors with specialized backgrounds. From this comes a well-crafted skein of information that's approachable, readable, followable, and—of course—executable. His excellent introduction to Chapter 6 reaffirms how the book should be used: "this book doesn't propose a linear, all-encompassing creative process to replace your preferred acting or directing technique. Rather, this book offers independent lessons that aim to help you ask more productive questions earlier in your creative process."

This book is meant for you. Pick it up. Find the tool, insight, or entire arc you need right now to make your work with these dynamic pieces of dramatic literature stronger, more effective, and authentic. Doesn't matter if you're an actor, teacher, director, or designer. Kevin helps you engage with the text, serving both the story and the form the story is riding on. It empowers you to reach beyond any hesitancy of doing Shakespeare right, or even being funny.

Shakespeare has given you excellent characters, in excellent stories with the unique melodies and rhythms to help ground and lead you. Kevin's book lights the way to explore it all and backs your play with simplicity and potency.

Sean Boyd
University of Nevada, Las Vegas

Acknowledgements

Thank you to my entire family. To Hannah and Grace, my father Cliff, my siblings Joe and Paige, and my mother, Sandy, who lent me her *Complete Works* all those years ago. I miss you every day.

A special thank you to Sean Boyd for writing the foreword to this book and for his thoughtful, expert feedback on this text, particularly concerning breath and its relationship to rhythm and communion. Extra special thanks to Sara Romersberger for all those exciting, expanding, and laughter-filled conversations about Shakespeare's clowns and fools in the early 2000s. I am deeply grateful for your camaraderie and encouragement.

I've been fortunate to learn from outstanding teachers, some of whom I will mention now. In particular, John Basil, who showed me the joys of Shakespeare, inspired my curiosity, and taught me to act boldly and truthfully in such rich, athletic language. Also, thank you to Rocco Dal Vera, who, early in my education, encouraged me to deepen my relationship with language.

Thank you to Avner Eisenberg, Julie Goell, Joan Mankin, and Diane Wasnak for teaching me to clown; and thank you to Fabio Mangolini, Antonio Fava, Ole Brekke, and Joan Schirle, for teaching me Commedia. Also, thank you to Jim Wise and Brant Pope, who taught me to embrace the moment, my instincts, and my common sense. Special thanks to José Quintero, whose teaching inspired me not only to improve my craft but to bring passion and embrace artistry within that craft.

Thank you to all my colleagues at Elon University. Special thanks to Kirby Wahl and Libby Purcell for their notes, fresh perspective, and encouragement mid-process. You got me over the hump. Also, thanks to Scott Proudfit, Susanne Shawyer, Fred Rubeck, Jade Arnold, and my partner in pedagogy, Kim Shively. Also, special thanks to Richard Rand, Davis Robinson, and Bruce Brockman for their encouragement and guidance over the years. Thank you to Stacey Walker, Lucia Accorsi, and the entire team at Routledge for making this idea a reality.

Thank you to all my students and fellow practitioners over the years. I am inspired by and learn from each of you. I must mention Griffin Todd in particular, whose interest and curiosity for Shakespeare's comedies and clowns inspired me in the early stages of conceiving this book.

Last but certainly not least, thank you to my partner, poet, astronomer, and avid Cure fan, Claudine Moreau, for her love and encouragement throughout the writing of this book. Your passion for life and language, and your love for the wonder of the universe, are ongoing inspirations . . . and not just on Fridays.

Introduction and Foundations

One

INTRODUCTION

This book aims to be a practical guide for twenty-first-century directors and actors. I've written it to serve practitioners, though it will also be of interest to Shakespeare educators, students, scholars, and enthusiasts. My hope for practitioners is that it will be both illuminating and practical in pre-production as well as during the rehearsal process. This book is for people wanting to better understand and utilize Shakespeare's comedic dramaturgy—the structure, assumptions, and traditions that influenced the entire comedic event—and how that knowledge can be synthesized with contemporary acting and directing techniques. My hope for practitioners and students is that it will help you create compelling, funny, and believable performances that are both impactful and accessible for today's audiences.

Shakespeare is one of the most widely produced playwrights in the world, and his comedies, when done well, have frequently transcended any present time to satisfy their audiences. The stories, characters, and language can be delightful, and some of his comedies have proven themselves effective even under radical interpretations. But Shakespeare's comedies also pose unique challenges.

Comedy can be an incredibly topical form of commentary, expression, and release, as it holds human folly up for

DOI: 10.4324/9781003273967-1

ridicule. But what was considered funny even just thirty years ago can be seen today as meaningless, obscure, or even offensive. Comedy's intended impact can change quickly with time, and Shakespeare's comedy isn't immune to this.

There are numerous books on Shakespeare's life, theatre, plays, and comedies. Sadly, however, these books are rarely written with practitioners in mind. They are simply too long and too detailed for most actors and directors to use while under the pressures of production. For the information in these books to be practical in a conventional setting, two things need to occur. First, the dramatically useful information needs to be distinguished from less applicable information so that we're not overwhelmed by the enormity of it. Second, this useful information needs to be presented in a way that can be readily synthesized with a practitioner's technique so that it can be effectively rehearsed and realized in performance.

This book does that. It distills useful information and pairs it with practical techniques through select key lessons. These key lessons function as both keys to unlock doors of deeper understanding and possibility, as well as becoming "key stones" in the construction of your performance or production. They also pair well with most contemporary acting techniques. Learning them will help you ask yourself more productive questions earlier in your creative process, leading you to a more thorough understanding of the script and its possibilities. They'll also help you learn new techniques or improve your existing skills for directing and performing Shakespeare's comedies. The key lessons in this book are additions—not substitutions—to the acting and directing process you already use.

This book is not comprehensive. It doesn't attempt to cover everything. It also assumes that the reader has a basic familiarity and appreciation for Shakespeare, comedy, and modern performance techniques.

In the chapters that follow, we'll begin with three comic traditions that had a profound impact on Shakespeare's writing. This will help us better perceive how he constructed his comedies and, likely, the impact he sought to achieve. After that, we'll borrow from the world of Clown, experiencing how these physical techniques and performance sensibilities can unlock our imaginations and help us find possibilities within Shakespeare's writing. Then we'll take a turn toward comedic avenues within Shakespeare's language. We'll finish by putting it all together in a selection of character studies that illuminate how these lessons can manifest in pre-production, rehearsal, and performance. At the end of each chapter, I've included a summary of key takeaways and, at times, cautions for practitioners on common traps and pitfalls.

When a production or performance falls short in the professional theatre, the cause of the failure can often be traced to interpretive mistakes rather than to errors in directorial or performance technique. With Shakespeare's comedies, two blunders that can hinder practitioners are:

1. An incomplete understanding of Shakespeare's comedic design. This is when the practitioners haven't fully recognized the dramaturgy—the comedic assumptions and traditions within the script—and, as a result, cannot fully capitalize on them.
2. A lack of awareness of the likely impact Shakespeare intended for his audience. This is when practitioners either miss some of the humor or have lost sight of where Shakespeare was trying to take his audience emotionally at that point in the story.

Having new knowledge, awareness, and skills will help you craft more satisfying performances and have a more profound impact on your audiences.

LAYING THE FOUNDATION

For the key lessons to be most effective, we need to establish a shared foundation of knowledge. We'll establish that foundation brick by brick in the rest of this chapter. These foundational bricks may initially read a little disjointed, but you'll see how they work together to establish a solid base for the remainder of the book.

THE GREAT CHAIN OF BEING

Awareness of the Great Chain of Being is a critical tool for better recognizing Shakespeare's dramatic design. Christian medieval Europe was somewhat obsessed with categorizing the contents of the world. They saw it as a way of understanding God's intentions. Given the hardships and periodic chaos everyday people had to contend with, such as disease, famine, and war, it's easy to understand why this appealed to them. The historic drawings that illustrate this Great Chain show God at the top. Under God, we find saints and angels, and, beneath them, layers of nobility. Beneath the nobility, you'll see everyday people, often depicted in the middle of the chain where they're equally pulled between Heaven and Hell. Beneath everyday people, you see classification of animals, then insects, then plants, then demons, and, finally, at the very bottom of the chain, the Devil. It's easy to imagine how this could influence a person's point of view on themselves and on other segments of society. In this pre-democratic paradigm, it was easy for the powerful to reflexively view people in lower socioeconomic situations as inferior. It's also easy to imagine how everyday people might view the powerful as their "betters."

Like most of Renaissance Europe, Elizabethan society was stratified and rigid by contemporary Western standards. It was a time when people were expected to know their place and keep their place. In addition to helping to maintain medieval power structures, this was seen as people accepting God's design, similar to what we see in the Great Chain of Being. This helps us better understand where Shakespeare's audience saw each character in a play on the chain and where they believed that a character should remain in order to keep the Great Chain intact.

An Elizabethan audience generally accepted that obeying this order was good and defying it was bad. It was largely understood that if one complied with the Great Chain, one was more likely to lead a peaceful life in a prosperous society with a pleasant afterlife to follow. They also thought the opposite was true. If a person defied and broke the Great Chain, then unnatural and evil things could happen to them and to society here and in the afterlife. This was connected to that society's predominant Christian faith. Whether a person's expression of that faith was genuine or performative was largely irrelevant; the expectation of belief was preeminent throughout Elizabethan society. When Macbeth murders King Duncan and becomes king even though he is not the rightful heir, then the Great Chain has been broken, and the kingdom will not return to peace and prosperity until it's been restored.

This is not to say that Shakespeare always validated or even conformed with this worldview; one can see where he subtly deviates from it. Still, understanding this concept of a Great Chain helps us imagine what Shakespeare's audience likely expected. We can then more fully recognize where

Shakespeare conforms or deviates from that expectation. That helps us recognize the impact he intended on his audience.

IMPORTANT CONVENTIONS AND REALITIES OF SHAKESPEARE'S THEATRE

Some general knowledge about the Elizabethan stage—its economic realities as well as select performance conventions—can help us better imagine how Shakespeare envisioned his plays being performed.

First, it's important to understand that the theatre of Shakespeare's day was a true people's theatre. A wide cross section of Elizabethan society regularly attended the theatre expecting to be entertained. Because of that reality, Shakespeare wrote plays to entertain multiple demographics. His plays contain humor for working people, the young and old, as well as relatable humor for merchants, aristocrats, and academics. He wanted his plays to be popular and commercially successful, so within his stories he regularly includes something for everyone. When we create theatre that entertains multiple audiences today, we're honoring one of Shakespeare's intentions as a dramatist.

Visualizing an Elizabethan theatre space can add insight into how Shakespeare expected his plays to be staged. If you can, do a quick internet search for images of Shakespeare's Swan Theatre; this is one of the theatres where Shakespeare was originally staged. It's likely that the famous 1596 drawing by Johannes de Witt will appear. As you look at that image, note the numerous acting spaces. The size of the large playing space, the relatively intimate balcony, the slightly larger area underneath that balcony known as the inner below, and the two large doors in the back wall where actors could enter and exit the space. It can be useful for us to imagine how one of Shakespeare's plays may have utilized this space as we shape our modern interpretation.

You'll also note the thrust configuration of the stage, which brought the audience into closer proximity with the actors. Some modern proscenium theatres may have the first row of audience twenty feet from the proscenium window, but the Elizabethan theatre was more intimate. Some audience members would even sit on the stage.

It's critical for modern practitioners to keep in mind that Elizabethan plays were frequently performed in the afternoon, outdoors, and on a generally bare wooden platform. Even when performed indoors, there were very few scenic elements. Instead, Elizabethan theatre evoked the audience's imagination by using spoken decor. Spoken decor is when the writer uses character dialogue to tell the audience what they should imagine on the stage. For example, in *A Midsummer Night's Dream*, Demetrius says, "Thou toldst me they were stolen into this wood." This line tells the audience to imagine a forest. When we stage a production conceived to evoke the audience's imagination, we are honoring another of Shakespeare's intentions as a dramatist.

Natural light was the predominant lighting source in Shakespeare's day. These plays were written to be performed outside, and electricity and gas lighting were not yet in use. Blackouts as we understand them today were impossible. Our current convention of having stagehands dressed in black moving scenery into place in near darkness hadn't been invented yet. Keeping this in mind can create opportunities for actor-driven comic action, which we'll see in future chapters.

Ultimately, it is the actors that embody Shakespeare's comedic design. In the Elizabethan theatre, the core acting company usually existed before the play was written. So, Shakespeare could write a play to serve a particular company of actors and maximize a particular actor's performance strengths. When we can discern which actor Shakespeare was likely writing a role for, and know that actor's skill set, then we've found another avenue for gaining insight into the playwright's intent.

Shakespeare's actors had to work quickly too. The economic realities of that theatre necessitated a short rehearsal process. It's important to understand that at this point in Western theatre history rehearsals were run more on a master–apprentice model. Directors, as we understand them now, did not exist. The job had not yet been invented. Actors had to look for performance guidance from within their scripts. Written stage directions were rare, but the playwright could influence the staging of their play by writing stage directions into the actual dialogue. This is known as embedded stage directions. For example, in *As You Like It*, when the character Silvius says, "If thou hast not sat as I do now," this is a very clear direction from the writer for the actor to sit.

ACTING: BUILDING ON YOUR CONTEMPORARY TECHNIQUE

In my first book on acting, *Applied Meisner for the 21st-Century Actor*, co-written with my colleague, Kim Shively, we discuss Sanford Meisner's definition of acting and its implications. Meisner stated that "Acting is living truthfully under imaginary circumstances," and this is worth fully understanding because of the guidance it provides to the actor and director about what acting is and—also useful—what acting is not. Understanding and embodying this definition helps us better interpret and perform contemporary roles, particularly in a realistic style. I've included that chapter in the Appendix of this book.

However, when acting and directing Shakespeare's comedies, we need to enhance this definition with two key adjustments:

1. the importance of expertise;
2. the importance of the audience.

These enhancements help us more effectively perceive Shakespeare's comedic design, and they'll also guide us in building upon our contemporary technique.

ENHANCEMENT 1: EXPERTISE

In Europe, after centuries of legally mandated amateurism, the theatre became professional again, just prior to the Renaissance. This professionalization took place for both scripted and unscripted plays; many scripts survive. The unscripted performances did not survive to the same degree, but a lot of what we now call Commedia dell'arte continued. This unscripted, improvisational style of performance was immensely popular throughout Europe. We also know that their expertise was perceived and purchased by consumers, hence the term "arte." This acknowledged playmaking as a profession, a trade similar in some ways to weavers and blacksmiths. An Elizabethan audience expected to see experts perform in both scripted and unscripted plays.

This is different than what we typically expect in contemporary realism. Generally, in realism, an actor is acting well if the audience can suspend their disbelief and forget they're watching an actor—feeling more like a fly on the wall watching events unfold in real life than like a person in a theatre being entertained. We have reality TV, where "real people" are put into extreme situations with the cameras rolling. In Shakespeare's theatre, this level of naturalism would have been insufficient. A Renaissance audience expected expertise from craftspeople. When they bought woven goods, they expected them to be of higher quality than what they could make at home. Same with their playmakers. From their perspective, if most anyone can speak words, then actors should speak poetry in a way that is better and more entertaining than what they regularly heard from everyday people. Same with singing, destroying a letter, or even something as mundane as putting on shoes. Today, we still hold this expectation for some styles of performance such as musicals, where the level of skill should be greater than an amateur can do at home. In Shakespeare's day, actors were expected to be entertaining and to behave with higher levels of expertise onstage than one typically saw in everyday life.

ENHANCEMENT 2: THE AUDIENCE IS THERE

Shakespeare did not incorporate a fourth wall as we understand it today. Whether a particular performance was staged in an outdoor or indoor theatre, the audience and actors were in almost the same light. This is known as universal lighting. It would have appeared absurd to ignore the audience that the actors could see in plain sight. Our contemporary convention of putting the audience in darkness and behaving like they aren't there hadn't been invented yet. Sanford Meisner, like many teachers of modern acting, didn't mention the audience in his definition of acting. But in Shakespeare's comedies it's generally useful to acknowledge the presence of the audience. This is easier said than done. "Acknowledge the audience" is simple to read but takes practice to effectively do; there are several nuances and serious traps to avoid when employing this idea in today's theatre. We'll get into all of that later in this book.

These two enhancements, expertise and the presence of the audience, are not universally important to each character at every moment in Shakespeare's comedies. Characters that directly address the audience or have overt presentations of skills should embrace these enhancements more frequently and fully. But from this point forward, consider this our definition of acting when grappling with Shakespeare's comedies: "Acting is living expertly under imaginary circumstances for the pleasure of your audience."

In the lessons that follow, you'll see how these two enhancements help us discover opportunities to more fully implement Shakespeare's comedic dramaturgy.

BELIEVABLE, BUT NOT REALISTIC

An audience will accept nonrealism as believable as long as the performance is consistent in establishing and following its own performance conventions. We see this regularly in musicals where singing and dancing are accepted as typical styles of communication. We also see this in slapstick violence where characters can recover from severe injuries and horrendous beatings in mere seconds. Take care not to unintentionally limit yourself when creating your role or directing your production. A great place to look for guidance in comedy are North American cartoons such as *SpongeBob SquarePants*. In these cartoons, the world is not realistic but it's consistent and therefore remains believable to its audience. In the first *SpongeBob SquarePants* film, the title character showers by ingesting soap and then sticking a hose into himself to push now-soapy water out of his entire sponge body. That is not realistic, but it's entertaining, and the audience accepts it as believable as they enjoy SpongeBob's bathing expertise. Anyone can shower, but only SpongeBob—the expert—is so thoroughly cleansed.

KEY TAKEAWAYS

- This book distills useful knowledge and presents key lessons that are helpful to twenty-first-century practitioners.
- The Great Chain of Being influenced how Shakespeare's audience perceived the characters and actions in a play. It influenced their expectations.
- When we create theatre that entertains multiple audiences and deliberately provokes their imaginations, we're honoring two of Shakespeare's intentions as a dramatist.
- Shakespeare usually wrote for a company of actors. It's helpful to assume he knew the actor for whom he was creating the role.
- Parts of the performance should demonstrate expertise.
- The audience is there. The fourth wall as we understand it today did not exist.
- Try not to limit your creativity by mistaking realism for believability. If the production is consistent, your audience will perceive nonrealistic choices as believable.

Under the Commedia Influence

Two

INTRODUCTION

It's useful for twenty-first-century practitioners to understand some of Shakespeare's major comic influences. This will help us ask more productive questions earlier in the creative process. This chapter and the next distills some important information and will help you do three things:

1. to more fully recognize Shakespeare's comedic dramaturgy;
2. to more fully understand Shakespeare's intended impact on his audience;
3. to discover more opportunities for creative, informed choices that are justified within Shakespeare's writing.

Commedia dell'arte had a significant impact on Shakespeare's writing, particularly in the first third of his career. One reason Shakespeare was so popular in his time was because he understood his audience. As a result, he was able to please them. When we understand what Shakespeare's audience expected, we better understand the impact Shakespeare likely intended. Though we aren't obligated to comply with his comedic intentions, it's helpful for us to understand them even should we chose to deviate from them.

DOI: 10.4324/9781003273967-2

Today, Commedia continues to provide creative stimulation for contemporary directors, and it's not uncommon for a Commedia-based concept to be applied to a Shakespeare play. The intersect between Shakespeare and Commedia dell'arte remains an area of interest for contemporary performance scholars as well.

COMMEDIA DELL'ARTE AND AUDIENCE EXPECTATIONS

This style of performance and play creation was very popular throughout Renaissance Europe. Sometimes referred to as the Italian comedy, Commedia dell'arte presented plays in a style that utilized character masks, physical comedy known as lazzi, improvisation, and identifiable stock characters such as the miserly old man and the clever servant. Commedia was physical, funny, and relatable. It pleased its audience.

Here's a brief description of a typical Commedia comic plot. It'll probably sound familiar. The two young lovers, traditionally heterosexual teenagers, are in love with each other. They want to get married, but one or both parents do not want them to be together and work to prevent their love and marriage. One parent might even want their teenage daughter to marry a different man, such as the Captain. The young lovers, however, assisted by the servants, overcome these parental obstacles by design and hilarious coincidence. The good are ultimately rewarded, and the bad are punished. The young lovers can now be together with the promise of marriage to follow at the end of the play.

This plot is alive and well in contemporary entertainment. It's also the basic plot skeleton we see in some of Shakespeare's plays. *The Two Gentlemen of Verona*, *A Midsummer Night's Dream*, and *Romeo and Juliet* all begin with a typical Commedia plot. Even after these plays diverge from this classic storyline, it's as if they're trying to get back onto that track. When Shakespeare deviates from this well-known narrative, he's likely playing with his audience's expectations in order to surprise and entertain them.

In addition to this typical Commedia plot, Elizabethan audiences were able to easily identify numerous Commedia stock characters based on their masks and mannerisms. Audiences of the time were accustomed to interpreting visual iconography, and they brought that understanding to a play. They still do this today. Contemporary audiences can easily identify twenty-first-century "types" such as geeks, jocks, and goths based on costumes, mannerisms, dialogue, and typical physical and verbal humor associated with these kinds of characters.

Understanding Commedia dell'arte helps us clearly perceive a "universe" of characters that Shakespeare's audience was familiar with viewing. When the audience recognizes a stock character, they begin to expect certain lines of comic business from that character. Today, we might expect a joke related to computers or comic books from a "geek" type. The Elizabethans likely expected a joke related to age or excessive thrift from the miserly, old Pantalone, or something surprisingly clever from the servant Arlecchino.

There are literally hundreds of individuated Commedia characters, and they can generally be categorized as falling into one of four main categories. In order of social status from highest to lowest, these four archetypes are:

1. old men (Pantalone and Doctore)
2. captains (Capitano)
3. lovers (Inamorati)
4. servants (Zanni)

Commedia gives us important interpretive tools for more clearly seeing Shakespeare's comedic design and an Elizabethan audience's expectations.

MASTERS AND SERVANTS

There is a status hierarchy within the Commedia universe. It can be helpful to think of this as a simplified chain of being. In this hierarchy, the wealthy and most powerful are on the top, and the poor and least powerful are at the bottom. This status hierarchy is divided into two large groups: masters and servants. In the Commedia universe, a character is one or the other, and there are different levels of status within those main groups. Regardless of where a character falls within this hierarchy, all Commedia characters are regularly stupid and inadvertently brilliant.

Masters have wealth and status. These are the merchants, doctors, captains, and the lovers. A master may command any servant, not only the servants in their employ. It's their collective job to employ the servants and provide for their minimal needs: a place to sleep (even if outside) and enough food not to starve. Masters typically try to provide their servants with as little as possible. It's important for the actors playing any master in the Commedia universe to understand that it's a master's obligation to punish their servants when the servants are wrong or threaten the status hierarchy. In the Commedia, like in the medieval and Renaissance Europe from which it sprang, anarchy leads to significant widespread suffering. Therefore, from a master's perspective, punishing servants when they do wrong prevents anarchy and contributes to the greater good.

All working people are lumped together as servants, and the low-status servant, Zanni, were the first characters in the

Commedia. They have the deepest roots in this style, and the audience should empathize with them and cheer them on. Servants are often more perceptive and wiser than their bosses, and their lack of power and status makes them more likely to suffer the repercussions of a master's poor decisions. Often attached to a particular higher-status character, like the nurse to Juliet in *Romeo and Juliet*, a servant has two jobs: obey the master and anticipate their needs. Servants typically try to get as much from the master as possible without destroying the master physically or financially. As uncomfortable as being a servant can be, in Renaissance Europe it was much better to be an employed servant than an unemployed servant. Without an effective social safety net, the unemployed could starve. Servants generally accept that they can be commanded and punished by any master, not just their particular employer. A servant never enjoys being punished. It's important that a threat of punishment from a master be a deterrent for the servant.

COMMEDIA STATUS HIERARCHY

At the very top of the Commedia status hierarchy is the Old Man Pantalone, a miserly, libidinous, old merchant who is often father to the young female lover. Just beneath Pantalone in status is another old man, the Doctore, a pompous know-it-all doctor or know-it-all teacher. Perpetually hungry and prone to lengthy monologues of Latin-peppered nonsense, it's all an attempt to overcompensate for his very limited learning. He's often the father to the young male lover. Below these old men in status are the captains. These braggart and often cowardly military men provide complications within the story, often by seeking marriage with Pantalone's daughter, the young female lover. They are often foreigners, folks from out of town or out of country. Then we have the young female and male lovers, the masters with the lowest status in this hierarchy. They are in love with the idea of being in love. They are virginal perfectionists, narcissistic, and accustomed to a nice lifestyle, but they have no real power. Their luxury depends on their parents' wealth.

Below the masters in status—and, as already mentioned, core to any Commedia story—are the servants. There are layers of status within the servant category. Indoor servants generally have more status than outdoor servants. It's common within Commedia that those with the lowest status are the smartest characters onstage, and no two servants can have the same status. Female servants tend to be slightly smarter than their male counterparts. This gendered status dynamic can be intriguing and very entertaining, even today. Life remains hard for many working people, but then as now, life was even harder for women. Surviving with dignity could be a challenge, and we can see that challenge frequently reflected in Shakespeare's comedies as well.

The Commedia status hierarchy promises dramatic harmony when honored and bodes discord and punishment when broken. In the Commedia universe, it is considered natural for people to be in love with people of similar age and socioeconomic class. It's only when a character is with their "natural" romantic match—the young with the young, old with the old, servants with servants, masters with masters, etc.—that the world can function harmoniously. The young bourgeois Juliet is in love with the young bourgeois Romeo, not with the servant Peter. When Shakespeare deviates or hints at deviating from this typical Commedia hierarchy, he's often doing so to surprise—and therefore entertain and please—his audience.

TITLES OF ADDRESS ARE IMPORTANT

In Elizabethan society, the use of titles and respect for them helped to maintain the social order and, from their view, the Great Chain of Being. Dramatically, they help to maintain the status hierarchy. These titles can help us unlock a deeper understanding of the given circumstances and therefore inspire physical expression and action. Titles can range from "sirrah" to "dread sovereign" and multiple layers in between. Titles help us open interpretive doors.

For example, in Act 3, scene 5 of Much Ado about Nothing, Constable Dogberry addresses Leonato as both "sir" and "your worship" when he informs Leonato that he, along with Verges and the Watch, have made an arrest. This creates an opportunity for lazzi, especially considering Dogberry's comedic function. A lazzi is a precise physical comedic bit that'll be explained in more detail shortly. For the director of the play as well as the actor playing Dogberry, expressing "your worship" differently than "sir" gives that actor opportunity to use their expertise to develop both justified and entertaining lazzi. If Dogberry bows to Leonato when using both those titles, how do the bows differ? Perhaps one is absurdly deeper than the other. Even in the histories and tragedies, where physicalized gags surrounding titles aren't always appropriate, expressing "your royal highness" differently than "sovereign" makes the performance and production that much more specific. To physicalize these two different titles as if they were identical in meaning ignores this opportunity for lazzi and likely makes the performance more general and predictable as a result.

TWO MAJOR COMMEDIA PERFORMANCE TRADITIONS

It's important to understand two common Commedia performance conventions employed in Shakespeare's plays.

LAZZI

Lazzi, as mentioned earlier, are physical-comedy sequences that have been rehearsed to a high level of precision. They are sometimes referred to as gags or bits. Periodic embodiment of expertise (lazzi) can help a production transcend realism into a more theatrical style while remaining plausible within the given circumstances. Lazzi can be short or long, simple or complicated. It's usually best if they're performed with the actors light on their feet rather than making unnecessary sounds with heavy footfalls.

Below is an example of a short lazzi about looking for a pen when it's behind your ear.

> Sitting at your office desk, you have the impulse to write a note to yourself on a piece of paper.
>
> You pull the paper closer and then reach for the pen on your desk. You discover the pen isn't where you thought it was.
>
> You begin to search your desk for where the pen has disappeared to. You look left, right, and behind your computer monitor.
>
> You see your hat on your desk and lift it up to see if the pen is underneath it.
>
> Holding the hat makes you think of your head. You then remember where you left the pen.
>
> You put down the hat and reach up to pull the pen from behind your ear.
>
> You react to the fact that it was behind your ear the whole time.
>
> You then write yourself the note on the piece of paper.

Below is an example of a longer lazzi; this one the famous Commedia fly lazzi. Here the servant Arlecchino is so hungry that he captures a fly and eats it. Individuated for each actor, the fly lazzi can entertain audiences for ten minutes or longer. There have been thousands of fly lazzi over the centuries; this is only one option.

> Establish that you're hungry. Dramatize how empty your belly is and the sounds that it is making. Show us that your ribcage resembles a xylophone.
>
> Fantasize about eating the most delicious stew in the world. What are the ingredients? After a quick imaginary trip to the market, show us how you'd prepare the vegetables, the starch, and the meat. You are of course very, very hungry, so your preparations become chaotic and overly enthusiastic as you dramatize slicing make-believe vegetables and roasting make-believe meat. Feel free to snack on bits of it as you mix it all into an enormous make-believe pot.
>
> Discover the fly. The stew fantasy fades away as you become increasingly mesmerized by the real fly. Track the fly.
>
> Trap the fly. How might you lure the fly to its death to satisfy your hunger? Maybe the first two attempts fail, and you succeed on the third. Now you have it!
>
> Play with it, perhaps like a housecat with a rodent it has caught.
>
> Slaughter and prepare the fly to be consumed. Pull off its wings, pull out the entrails, and in other ways prepare it for consumptions.
>
> Consume it. All at once or in courses, each bit more satisfying that the last. Share that satisfaction with the audience.
>
> Maybe after the satisfaction of consuming the fly, there's a complication: you discover it's alive inside of you! It flies

> from one end of your stomach to the other, pulling you
> around the stage, jerking you from point to point. When you
> feel that it's about to burst through your stomach wall like
> something from the movie Alien, you work to barf it up, and
> it escapes out your mouth. Or maybe that doesn't work,
> and you have bear down to fart it out your ass. The fly then
> escapes down your pant leg, flies three feet, and dies from
> the nasty smell, dropping dead on the ground. You consider
> eating it anyway. Maybe you do.

Even very short lazzi can entertain and please the audience. They give the actor opportunity to embody expertise within the imaginary world of the play. Lazzi showcases skill.

TIRADE

A tirade is a long monologue where the character builds a rant or in other ways escalates their passions to a crescendo. A servant might build a tirade about their hunger or terrible working conditions. A lover could rant on the topic of love or how their lover doesn't sufficiently love them because they don't style their hair properly. A captain might bluster about his bedroom exploits while trying to conceal his cowardice on the battlefield. Pantalone might hold forth on the laziness of his servants and how those ingrates want a raise. The tirade is frequently used in our contemporary comedies as well.

Lazzi and tirades can sometimes combine. Julia's famous "hateful hands" speech from *The Two Gentlemen of Verona* is a great example. Here the character can rant her regrets about tearing up the letter while acting it out in lazzi.

> Oh hateful hands, to tear such loving words;
> Injurious wasps, to feed on such sweet honey,

And kill the bees that yield it, with your stings;
I'll kiss each several paper, for amends:
Look, here is writ, kind Julia: unkind Julia,
As in revenge of thy ingratitude,
I throw thy name against the bruising stones,
Trampling contemptuously on thy disdain.
And here is writ, love wounded Protheus.
Poor wounded name: my bosom, as a bed,
Shall lodge thee till thy wound be thoroughly healed;
And thus I search it with a sovereign kiss.
But twice, or thrice, was Protheus written down:
Be calm (good wind) blow not a word away,
Till I have found each letter, in the letter,
Except mine own name: that, some whirlwind bear
Unto a ragged, fearful, hanging rock,
And throw it thence into the raging sea.
Lo, here in one line is his name twice writ:
Poore forlorn Protheus, passionate Protheus:
To the sweet Julia: that I'll tear away:
And yet I will not, sith so prettily
He couples it, to his complaining names;
Thus will I fold them, one upon another;
Now kiss, embrace, contend, do what you will.

MAJOR COMMEDIA ARCHETYPES AND TYPICAL LINES OF COMIC BUSINESS

Noting the Commedia archetype within Shakespeare's individuated characters can help us ask productive questions earlier in the creative process. It's also helpful to note when the story conforms or deviates from the conventional Commedia plot. Below is a brief description of some of the comic business associated with the major Commedia archetypes.

This list is not exhaustive; it's enough to get you started. Commedia dell'arte is immense, and it's easy to get lured into the enticing details. We'll stay focused on the main characters.

PANTALONE

Pantalone is at the top of the status chain. His body is old, but his mind is sharp. He is greedy and cheap; he would rather die than pay full price. He can be ruthless. He's also quite lusty and is often attracted to younger female characters such as the indoor female servant Columbina. His lust is not necessarily criminal or deviant. Neither is his greed; they're both motivated by his deep fear of death. He surrounds himself with youth and material things in order to mitigate that anxiety.

TYPICAL LINES OF COMIC BUSINESS
- Old man bending down to pick up a coin.
- Miser counting his money.
- Threatening to beat his servant(s).
- Bowel issues: he's constipated and suffering until the laxative kicks in, with hilarious results.
- Fears and fantasies about sexual performance.
- May compose a song or poem to woo a younger woman—may want to appear "hip."
- May rant to the audience about his child, situation, or servants, about how he became successful in business.

DOCTORE

An older man, though not typically as old as Pantalone. He compensates for his anxieties by pretending to be an authority on any subject. Addicted to feeling like an expert, he's a know-it-all, would-be expert on everything. A lot of what he presents as fact is absurdly false. He's a bullshitter.

TYPICAL LINES OF COMIC BUSINESS
- Peppers his speech with Latin and other foreign phrases.
- Always hungry for food. He can eat and eat and eat and never feel full.
- Lectures authoritatively about nonsense.
- Lectures authoritatively while trying to sell a person something. Echoes of "snake oil" and miracle elixir salesman.
- Traditionally portrayed with a large belly.

CAPITANO

Capitano is a braggart in peacetime and a coward on the battlefield. He will never fight. Middle-aged, he brags about his sexual exploits as well. Sometimes he is having an affair with Pantalone's wife. Sometimes he is the preferred would-be husband for Pantalone's daughter, even though she remains devoted and in love with her young male lover and never falls for the captain. Sometimes, the captain woos Pantalone's daughter as a way of facilitating his affair with Pantalone's wife. The captain is often a foreigner, and traditionally Spanish.

TYPICAL LINES OF COMIC BUSINESS
- Bragging: the battle résumé.
- Bragging: the sexual-exploit résumé.
- Outrageous lies related to the above.
- Preparing to fight physical lazzi (he will never fight).
- Sudden outbursts of extreme fear and cowardice, quickly covered with bravado.
- Has a relationship with his small, average, or large weapon, which he may have unintentionally sexualized. The weapon may have a name and battle résumé as well.

LOVERS

The lovers seek their happiness through the pursuit of idyllic, romantic love. They are dignified and intelligent except when emotionally unbalanced by their passions, at which point they become incredibly volatile and shallow narcissists. The characters are often teenagers, passionate, and emotionally immature. Lovers take themselves extremely seriously and have absolutely no sense of humor about themselves at all. They are compulsive about how "true love" should be expressed and received. They overreact when their expectations are not perfectly met. Also, young lovers can often feel the presence of their counterpart when that person enters the stage. They're like Jedi that way.

TYPICAL LINES OF COMIC BUSINESS

- Writing a letter, song, or poem to their beloved.
- Waiting for or receiving a letter, song, or poem from their beloved.
- Punishing their servant when disappointed with the above.
- Going totally "mad" with passion when their expectations aren't met.
- The ecstasy of touching their beloved.
- Planning or trying to kill themselves when they think their love affair is doomed, which is frequently.

SERVANTS

Servants rarely have enough of the bare essentials: food, sleep, and time. They are often in a hurry, either trying to complete their duties so they can have some extra time to sleep, eat, and flirt, or they're in a hurry trying to conceal some mishap in order to avoid being punished. As a rule, servants do not sit in the presence of the masters.

There are many different kinds of servants in the Commedia universe, and they can generally be classified as first or second Zanni. This classification is status-based and does not indicate a character's importance within the story. For example, one of the most significant comic duos in western theatre is the servant pair of Arlecchino (second Zanni) and Brighella (first Zanni). In this relationship, Arlecchino—perhaps the most beloved character in the Commedia—is the one with the lower status and typically the more innocent of the two. Brighella is more of an opportunist and is willing to bend the rules to get his needs met. He can hatch a foolproof plan that you know is going to backfire on them both.

The female servants are often the subject of unwelcome sexual advances from male characters, particularly from Pantalone who is often the female servant's employer.

TYPICAL LINES OF COMIC BUSINESS

- Lazzi related to eating, such as Arlecchino's famous fly lazzi.
- Lazzi related to sleeping and other everyday routines.
- Lazzi related to work.
- Mockery of their masters (behind their backs of course).
- Messages misdelivered.
- Plausible confusion over everyday tasks.
- Lazzi related to being punished or beaten. Overreact? Underreact? Fall asleep? Ass goes numb? Sips tea?

Noting the core Commedia archetype can spark ideas. For example, Don Armado from *Love's Labour's Lost* is built from a Capitano archetype. Perhaps there are places within that role where time-tested Capitano lazzi can inform the choices?

Where might the actor playing Armado showcase skill and please the audience in Capitano fashion?

Comic lines of business can sometimes be seen in Shakespeare's actual dialogue, such as with Julia's tirade and torn-letter lazzi mentioned earlier; or they can be simply alluded to because Shakespeare's actors and audience would have recognized the character's Commedia root and developed expectations for certain lazzi as a result. When we imagine the audience's expectations for a certain character and accept that Shakespeare wanted to please his audience by either conforming or deviating from those expectations, we can step into a larger world of justified comic possibilities. We'll see later in this chapter how this can inform more complex interpretive issues as well.

HYBRID CHARACTERS

Like many Renaissance writers, Shakespeare wrote individuated characters, particularly as he gained experience. These individuated characters are more sophisticated than a pure Commedia archetype. However, they often contain elements from one or more of the major Commedia stock characters outlined earlier. Again, recognizing the Commedia influence can inspire and guide us.

One example would be Benedick from *Much Ado about Nothing*—too old to be a "young" lover but a lover all the same. He also displays Capitano-like bragging without the cowardice. Malvolio in *Twelfth Night* is another example. Though an indoor servant in status, Malvolio frequently displays Doctore's snobbish, windbag sensibilities as he "baffles" Sir Toby, Viola, and others. In addition to being a savvy politician, Polonius possesses some Pantalone qualities.

Examining a character's Commedia roots—and how that particular character deviates from those roots—can help us discern how Shakespeare might be working on his audience's expectations.

COMMEDIA DELL'ARTE AND THE "CLAUDIO PROBLEM"

Let's take a look at a common problem when staging *Much Ado about Nothing*. In particular, the director and cast have a problem with the character Claudio. How can a modern audience continue to find Claudio likeable after he is so easily duped—twice—by the villain Don John and his henchmen and then mercilessly shames the innocent Hero on their wedding day? This can be a challenging justification issue for the actor playing Claudio. Why does Claudio readily trust a known villain? It's also a challenge for the director who likely wants their audience to celebrate rather than lament Claudio and Hero's ultimately successful courtship.

Unfortunately, this problem is exacerbated by the popularity of Kenneth Branagh's film version of the play, which we'll discuss shortly. But examining the "Claudio problem" through a Commedia lens is a useful start for helping the practitioners craft a reasonable, and ultimately forgivable, justification for Claudio's actions. It's the first step toward keeping Claudio likeable to a modern audience so that he can eventually be forgiven for his cruel actions toward Hero.

Branagh's enjoyable 1993 film makes the interpretive choice that the core characters are all aware of Claudio and Hero's mutual affection from the beginning of the story. We see this with the various nods and knowing smiles at the top of the film as Leonato reads the letter announcing Don Pedro's victory at battle and imminent arrival with Claudio and the rest of his entourage. This behavior creates a reality where Claudio and Hero's mutual affection is as openly known as the "merry war" between Benedick and Beatrice.

Upon examination, though, we can see that this choice is not supported by Shakespeare's text. It also makes the "Claudio problem" more difficult to overcome. While the battle of wits between Beatrice and Benedick is openly discussed in Shakespeare's dialogue, the characters say nothing about a love affair between Hero and Claudio.

In Act 1, you'll note that when Don Pedro first enters with Claudio, Benedick and the rest, that it is Don Pedro that first calls attention to Hero, "I think this is your daughter." He then talks with Leonato about Hero. For an Elizabethan audience, they would likely see Hero, the daughter of the wealthy and respected Leonato, as a possible match for the prince, Don Pedro, especially after a war when the prince would aim to strengthen alliances and replenish his treasury. Later in the same scene, Don Pedro reports that Leonato hopes "some occasion" may keep Don Pedro and his court at Leonato's longer than a month. If the audience views Hero and Don Pedro as natural matches at this point in the story, then this occasion would likely be their marriage. This scenario is in keeping with classic Commedia cultural expectations, where characters will seek their "natural" romantic counterpart. Hero is the highest status female character in the play. Don Pedro is the highest status male character. In the Commedia universe, they belong together.

Once alone, Claudio asks Benedick what he thinks of Hero. As Benedick banters with Claudio, there is no indication that he knows of Claudio's attraction to Hero. Later, Benedick presses Claudio for clarity, to make sure that Claudio is genuine with his affection for Hero. Soon Don Pedro returns, and Benedick quickly reveals Claudio's love for Hero. Don Pedro seems to give his blessing with "Amen, if you love her, for the lady is very well worthy." Claudio responds, "You speak this to fetch me in my Lord." Again, this is textual evidence that Hero is the natural match for Don Pedro. Claudio seems to think that he is not permitted to court Hero. This early exchange can establish Claudio's insecurity about pursuing a woman out of his league. This insecurity can later help us justify Claudio's duping by Don John's shallow schemes.

Claudio is written in a young-lover archetype. Lovers are insecure, super-serious about love, and crave perfection. Shakespeare paints a complicated situation at the top of the play where Claudio has fallen in love with the woman that most of the audience would see as the future wife of the prince Don Pedro. As these early scenes continue this is made abundantly clear when Don Pedro tells Claudio that he "will break with her" and after making sure that Hero returns Claudio's sentiments through his use of disguise that he will then "break" with her father Leonato. Further evidence of a general understanding that Don Pedro is Hero's intended match is provided in Act 2 prior to the masquerade party when Leonato says to Hero, "if the prince do solicit you in that kind, you know your answer." Hero does not verbally respond, but her cousin Beatrice soon says that "The fault will be in the music cousin, if you be not wooed in good time." Hero remains silent until the revelers enter. She does not voice agreement or refusal.

When addressing the "Claudio problem," it's helpful for us to pay attention to the text and understand that Claudio's affection for Hero is not well known. When looking at the dialogue, there are numerous lines that indicate that Don Pedro and Hero have been matched. Though both aristocrats, Claudio is not Don Pedro's equal in status. Also, there is no textual evidence to suggest that Hero and Claudio have had a serious conversation about their feelings or spoken about much of anything. Is Claudio confident that Hero returns his affection?

Recognizing the story's Commedia roots can help the actor playing Claudio fuel that deep insecurity about Hero, and justify that unrelenting feeling that he doesn't belong with her and that she would naturally seek a man of higher status. This creates a confirmation bias for Claudio and helps that actor justify succumbing to both the "prince woos for himself" and the "ruffian at the chamber window" schemes without necessarily being perceived as entitled, intensely jealous, and unforgivably paranoid.

If a modern audience can empathize with Claudio as an insecure young man who doesn't feel fully deserving of Hero's love, this can help to keep him sympathetic and ultimately forgivable. Finding the Commedia in Shakespeare can help us envision what Shakespeare's audience would likely have expected: Don Pedro as Hero's natural match. This helps us understand why Claudio can make such terrible mistakes.

CAUTION

Let the Commedia roots you find in a script inform but not dominate your choices. Shakespeare was influenced by Commedia dell'arte, and perceiving these roots can help us uncover avenues that both enhance the play's entertainment value and help us address thorny interpretive issues such as the "Claudio Problem." Still, Shakespeare was more interested in the humanity of individual characters and not just "types" of characters. Embrace that.

KEY TAKEAWAYS

- Shakespeare understood his audience and wrote to deliberately conform or deviate from their expectations.

- Shakespeare's audience was familiar with Commedia dell'arte characters, its plots, and its status hierarchy. This had an impact on what they expected from a play and its characters.
- Some of Shakespeare's characters have their roots in Commedia. Recognizing these roots can help us find useful avenues of comic business, even if the character's a hybrid.
- Master–servant relationships are dramatically useful.
- Titles of address can be clues to interpretive possibilities. Notice them and experiment with dramatizing them, especially if the title changes.
- Tirades and Lazzi are useful Commedia performance conventions. Recognizing those opportunities helps us better realize the script's performance possibilities.
- Understanding what Shakespeare's audience would consider a character's "natural" match can help us better perceive Shakespeare's comedic design.

Misrule and Fools

Three

INTRODUCTION

In addition to the Commedia dell'arte, there are two other comic traditions that had a major impact on Shakespeare's writing. These two traditions have their roots in medieval performance conventions, and they are woven tightly into Shakespeare's comedies. The Elizabethan audience was familiar with both and expected to see them in their theatre. These two traditions are Fool and Clown. It's useful for modern practitioners to understand them because it will help us find creative opportunities that are both supported in Shakespeare's text and justified by Elizabethan performance conventions.

In Shakespeare, the fool and the clown are particular kinds of characters that can inhabit a play in any genre. These roles are generally referred to as the stage clown. The stage clown is often listed simply as "Clo" or "Clown" in the folio scripts and was typically played by the principal comedian or head comic in a theatre troupe. The principal comedian was an important member of Shakespeare's theatre company.

Shakespeare wrote for two principal comedians during his career: first, William (Will) Kemp; second, Robert Armin. At different times they were both business partners with Shakespeare, and during their associations with Shakespeare would have regularly appeared in his plays. Understanding

DOI: 10.4324/9781003273967-3

the performance styles of both these actors, as well as the comic traditions they belonged to, can help us better realize these very demanding roles today.

The professional fool was a fairly common part of a noble's household. They were expected to sing, tell stories, perform acrobatics, and in other ways entertain the lord. We sometimes refer to them as jesters. There was also a version of this kind of fool that would frequent taverns and entertain a more working-class clientele. Professional fools wore a visually distinct costume when working—often a patched, motley coat—and sometimes employed the use of a bauble, a decorated baton usually with the likeness of a human head on one end of it.

The professional fool—who fools for their livelihood— stands in sharp contrast to the natural fool. The natural fool of that day was one who was born "foolish." This could apply not only to people whose sensibilities were simply a little quirky or peculiar, but also, unfortunately, to people with disabilities or who were disabled or neurologically diverse. Both kinds of fools appear in Shakespeare's plays, and there's reason to believe that both kinds were played by Robert Armin.

The clown, at that point, was also known as a rustic. In his book, *Shakespeare's Clown*, David Wiles describes the rustic as male, of low social status, written in ordinary prose, and one who is free to separate himself from the role and plot structure of the play; more on this last point soon. This rustic clown has its roots in the Lord of Misrule tradition, a regular, sometimes annual event, where the local ruler is temporarily replaced for a week or so by a commoner who is expected to rule in a ridiculous fashion, complete with hilarious and silly proclamations and even a court of misrule. Similar to present-day Mardi Gras in New Orleans, this tradition provided a defined period of time where everyday social norms were relaxed or suspended as the Lord of Misrule facilitated a festive, pleasurable anarchy. The rustic was also identifiable by their visually distinct costume as well as an unusual prop such as a wooden sword or comic scepter. These roles appear most frequently in the first half of Shakespeare's career and were often played by Will Kemp. We can say this with some certainty because in some quartos as well as the first folio, the clown role in certain plays is sometimes referred to as "Kemp." In the *Romeo and Juliet* first folio, for example, it actually says, "enter Will Kemp."

PRINCIPAL COMEDIAN FUNCTION

It helps the modern practitioner to know that in addition to being a character in the plot of Shakespeare's play, the principal comedian also serves a specific function within the dramatic event. It can be helpful to think of this function as similar to our understanding of protagonist and antagonist. In addition to being a character in the play, one of the functions of a play's protagonist is to be exceptional or special in some way, and to take action. One of the functions of the play's antagonist is to oppose that action. These functions are necessary to propel the story regardless of any particular character.

The principal comedian also has a function: to become the audience's avatar within the play. They serve as the viewer's empathetic bridge between the imaginary world of the play and the everyday world of the audience. In order to establish and maintain this bridge, as we noted from Wiles earlier, this actor had exceptional freedom to improvise within character and plot and also to step outside the narrative completely. This relationship is an important part of Shakespeare's comic dramaturgy. It's similar in some ways to contemporary circus, where the circus clown becomes the audience's representative and serves as an empathetic bridge between the magical world of an expert circus and the everyday world of the audience.

Similar to a circus clown, this principal comedian was also visually distinguished from the rest of the acting company by their costume. We've already mentioned this concerning the professional fool and rustic clown, but it's useful to remember that this was also a common convention in medieval religious theatre. The lead comics within those plays were regularly distinguished from the other characters by their often devil-like costumes. For an Elizabethan audience, this visual distinction was seen as something of a promise to provide comic relief.

Will Kemp and Robert Armin had different aesthetics, and each brought unique performance strengths and sensibilities to the stage. Because Shakespeare often had the advantage of writing for a known company of actors, he could write plays that capitalized on these strengths. Understanding these strengths can then help modern practitioners find comedic opportunities within Shakespeare's writing and take advantage of them for the pleasure of the audience. This is another key lesson in helping us recognize and advance Shakespeare's comedic design.

WILL KEMP

Will Kemp's go-to character was a rustic clown: a plain, working man of lower socioeconomic status, often from the country or in other ways from out of town. Prior to working with Shakespeare, Kemp was already a celebrity and had toured Continental Europe. He was a gifted improviser and outstanding dancer. He was known for having very muscular legs and exceptional leaping ability which he would showcase onstage. If one of Shakespeare's characters mentions their legs, there's a solid chance the role was written for Kemp. He was tall and could easily command the attention of the audience. Some of the roles we think Shakespeare wrote for him are Bottom, Dogberry, Falstaff, and Launce.

Kemp's performance style was marked by a relationship of equals between himself and the groundlings, people who could not afford a seat in the theatre and instead paid less to stand in the yard directly in front of the stage. Seen as a plain, working man, Kemp became that audience's representative onstage, having the experiences that working-class folks could only imagine. We see this in *A Midsummer Night's Dream* when Bottom the weaver, a worker, is magically transformed and has a love affair with the queen of the fairies. Many people fantasize about what it might be like to have a supernatural experience, or to hobnob with the powerful, the rich, and the famous. Kemp's Bottom shows us what could happen if our dreams came true, with hilarious results. This kind of relationship between performer and audience can also be seen in contemporary circus, where a clown attempts to replicate the expertise they've just seen performed in the ring. After seeing the expert tightwire act, the audience might be wondering if they could do that too, and the circus clown shows them what would happen to them on the wire, with hilarious consequences.

Kemp was a skilled physical comedian, and the root of his comedic style is in solo performance. Shakespeare would often write Kemp a scene or monologue within the first twenty minutes of the play where he could hold stage alone or nearly alone. This gave Kemp an opportunity to bond with his audience early; Launce in *The Two Gentlemen of Verona* is a prime example. Kemp's roles are sometimes marked by the use of a small supporting cast for Kemp to play off of, like in *Midsummer* between Bottom and the other Mechanicals.

Kemp was also known for improvisation. His performance style was likely front-of-mind when Hamlet advises the players to "let those who play your clowns, speak no more than is set down for them." When preparing a Kemp-based role, can you find the tension between the playwright's story and dialogue and the actor's desire to improvise and create havoc like a Lord of Misrule might do? Where does this principal comedian try to, and perhaps for a time succeed, in usurping the script? Where might it be helpful to unleash some chaos?

Also, many of Shakespeare's famous malaprops—characters that regularly use the wrong words to express themselves—were also written with Kemp in mind. This skillful and humorous misuse of language aligns with rustic-clown performance sensibilities, where a rural outsider comes to town and tries to use words they don't fully understand.

KEY TAKEAWAYS ON KEMP

- Identifiable by costume.
- Thrives holding stage alone.
- Relationship of equals with working-class groundling audience.
- Opportunities to improvise or appear to usurp the script.
- Opportunities to physicalize or in other ways show off their celebrity dancing and leaping ability.
- Malapropism.

ROBERT ARMIN

Shakespeare and Kemp had a falling-out in the late 1500s. Robert Armin then joined the acting company as principal comedian. This marked a decisive shift in Shakespeare's writing, likely because the performance styles of Kemp and Armin were quite different. Though it's impossible to know for certain what caused Shakespeare to modify his comedic writing, one sees a clear change beginning with *As You Like It*, and those changes correspond well with what we know of Armin's comic style. Recognizing these differences can help us better identify the performance opportunities within Shakespeare's comedic design.

Robert Armin was a celebrity professional fool and actor, well known prior to working with Shakespeare. Comfortable and experienced fooling at the tavern as well as at the palace, Armin was a sophisticated person and performer. In addition to being an actor and comedian, he was also a playwright and an author.

In his book, *Nest of Ninnies*, Armin makes observations on fools both professional and "natural." This distinction between the professional fool—one who fools skillfully for pay—and the natural fool—one who fools unintentionally without pay—is important to note when interpreting Shakespeare's comedies. You can see that distinction in some of the roles Shakespeare likely wrote with Armin in mind such as Caliban, Cloten, Feste, and Lear's Fool. In this list, Cloten and Caliban would be considered the natural fool. Though it's impossible to say with complete certainty that Armin played a certain role, David Wiles makes an excellent case in *Shakespeare's Clown*, particularly for Caliban. It's useful for us to accept the casting of Kemp or Armin as likely for certain roles because it helps the practitioners recognize performance opportunities within the script.

Armin's comic style often employed a higher-status relationship with his audience where it was made clear that the true fool was not him but the characters and audience members who thought themselves wittier than him. His professional fool characters often provide clever, humorous, and sometimes philosophical insight into the foolish actions taken by both major characters and humanity in general. An expert among the ignorant, his position as fool allows him to speak truth to power in a way that the average person in that day could not. We see this clearly in Twelfth Night when Feste proves Olivia the fool for over-mourning her deceased brother whose "soul is in heaven." The fool can periodically step outside of the established Elizabethan status hierarchy.

Armin's performance style is notably marked by mimicry and song. Does your character sing? Solid chance Armin played the role. If you are playing a role written for Armin, where are the opportunities for vocal mimicry? Feste sings multiple times during Twelfth Night. He also employs vocal mimicry to portray both himself and Sir Topas when tormenting Malvolio in the latter half of the play.

We can reasonably assume that Armin was unusual-looking. We know that he was shorter than average, and several of the characters he likely played are compared to animals. In contrast to the tall Kemp, who often held stage alone, Armin often worked as part of a trio, like Feste with Sir Toby and Sir Andrew in Twelfth Night. When Armin does hold stage alone for a longer period of time, his characters often do so in the second half of the play. Whereas Kemp forged a bond with his audience during his first contact with them, Armin seems to have been more effective bonding with his audience more gradually. He could then intensify and expand that connection as the play progressed.

KEY TAKEAWAYS ON ARMIN
- Identifiable by costume.
- Played both professional and "natural" fools.

- Higher-status relationship with the audience.
- Opportunities to sing and mimic.
- Often worked in a trio.

INTERTWINING TRADITIONS

In Shakespeare's comedies, these three major comic traditions—Commedia dell'arte, Clown, and Fool—frequently intertwine in ways that provide multiple, justifiable avenues for creativity. We can see this with a character like Feste. He is still a servant to the Countess Olivia while being a professional fool. In this way, the practitioner can justifiably utilize their understanding of professional fool, Armin's acting style, and the master–servant dynamics associated with Commedia while crafting the performance. A clown such a Launcelot Gobbo is still a servant to first Shylock and later Bassanio in *The Merchant of Venice*. For this role, practitioners are justified in crafting a performance inspired by the Rustic and Lord of Misrule traditions, Kemp's performance style, and Commedia-inspired master–servant dynamics.

We can also see these intertwining traditions embodied in different characters within a play itself. When capitalized on, this variety of traditions can heighten the range of dynamics onstage. For example, in *Love's Labour's Lost*, we see the rustic clown Costard, likely played by Kemp, sharing stage with the Commedia-inspired Holofernes, Don Armado, and Moth. Or in *The Tempest* where we see the "natural" fool Caliban, possibly played by Armin, hold stage opposite the professional fool Trinculo. Their styles are distinct, yet they can interplay to create a nuanced and more textured cohesive whole.

Lessons from the Clown World

Four

INTRODUCTION

Clarity is critical with theatre, comedy, and with Shakespeare in particular. Without clarity, it's very difficult for an audience to suspend their disbelief and give over to the comedic event. They're simply too busy being confused. The need for clarity extends beyond language and encompasses all of the actions onstage. Though clarity often begins with practitioners having a detailed comprehension of Shakespeare's rich language and the given circumstances their characters are living under, actors also need the ability to embody that understanding and communicate it to an audience behaviorally.

As we continue, let's keep in mind that a modern audience expects a high level of both believability and entertainment value in a performance. Shakespeare's comedic design helps us accomplish both these goals as we behave expertly in the imaginary world for the audience's pleasure. His text provides the time-tested "what" of the story—the plot, characters, dialogue, and such. The techniques in this chapter provide some clowning tools for the "how" of the story—the choices and actions that can be played with what Shakespeare's comedic design offers. These contemporary clown techniques and sensibilities also offer skill, structure, and vocabulary for the director guiding the actor during the creative process. We'll borrow and adapt those techniques and sensibilities in this

DOI: 10.4324/9781003273967-4

chapter. Toward the end of the chapter there's an example showing how all of these elements might work together.

CONTEMPORARY CLOWN

Clown is an incredibly useful set of skills for an actor performing in any style. It's both a noun and a verb—a kind of character but also actions. Clowns are vulnerable, adventurous, and possess common sense. Clowns are logical problem-solvers. Avner Eisenberg—who I will tell you more about shortly—defines clowning as "solving ordinary problems in unexpected ways."

Clowns are in direct contact with their audience and forge an empathetic bond with them. They engage "in the moment" with that particular audience as it exists right now: the interest of individual audience members, their laughter, their sneezing, and a host of other behaviors. The audience is the "other character" in a behavioral dialogue with the clown.

"Acting is reacting" is often heard while studying contemporary acting technique. Clowns also learn to react to the behavior of their audience. This is part of what we call "clowning." It's the moment-to-moment, action–reaction bridge between the everyday life of the audience viewing the event and the comedic event happening onstage.

The contemporary clown, like Shakespeare's principal comedian centuries earlier, has the liberty to periodically step outside of the status hierarchy. Like the principal comedian, today's clown can also step outside of the narrative altogether to comment on the action, deal with the audience's behavior, do something anachronistic, or simply take a short break. This is similar to the comic traditions that influenced Shakespeare and his audience's expectations.

Developing a direct, humorous, and empathetic relationship with an audience, however, is not exclusively the concern of the principal comedian. Other characters can also benefit from creating a bond with the audience, and many of Shakespeare's characters employ direct address. Just because Feste is the principal comedian's role in *Twelfth Night* doesn't mean that Malvolio doesn't establish a relationship with the audience. It's just that the specific function of Feste requires that his relationship with the audience be direct and empathetic enough to fulfil Shakespeare's comedic design—to become that humorous bridge.

WHAT ABOUT THE FOURTH WALL?

In live theatre, clowns don't typically perform with a fourth wall. It didn't exist in Shakespeare's theatre. Today, the fourth wall exists in films and in several theatrical styles, but contemporary clowns rarely employ one onstage.

In earlier chapters, we saw how the comic traditions that influenced Shakespeare—Commedia dell'arte, Clown, and Fool—cultivate and rely on a direct connection between actor and audience, where the actor is overtly talking with and reacting to the audience members. Shakespeare capitalized on this in his writing, particularly in the roles he created for Kemp and Armin. Removing the fourth wall in today's live theatre, or accepting that this separation doesn't actually exist, makes this connection possible.

The predominance of the fourth wall in modern acting can put us at a disadvantage when working on Shakespeare and other historical plays. The vast majority of modern acting techniques were developed to improve the actor's believability in realism. The pressure to appear "believable" continues to be paramount in the twenty-first century, and, as a result, conventional acting programs develop skills and sensibilities best suited to realism. This makes sense given that most actors will work the majority of their careers in realism. But for practitioners of the stage with Shakespeare's comedies, the techniques associated with realism are not sufficient to fully utilize Shakespeare's dramaturgy.

To realize those possibilities, modern practitioners need to embrace the function of the principal comedian by establishing a strong, empathetic, and enjoyable connection between the everyday world of the audience and the imaginary world of the play. We learn the immediacy and vulnerability of this connection in contemporary clown.

CLOWNS AND AUDIENCES

If you are performing in a conventional theatre company, your audience might be unaccustomed to having an actor directly clown with them. Most modern audiences reflexively expect a fourth wall. Even when a character stands isolated in a shaft of light delivering a monologue with an audience sitting in darkness, an exchange of actual impulsive behaviors between them doesn't always occur. If we're to fully inhabit Shakespeare's comedic design, we need a relationship with the audience that is more immediate and playful than this contemporary monologue convention.

This creates a challenge and opportunity for the actor that clowns: how to forge this bond with your audience. What is the process for establishing an open, enjoyable, and ongoing channel of rapport between audience and clown?

MEET THE AUDIENCE

In the previous chapter, we noted the different relationships Kemp and Armin established with their audiences. Allowing ourselves to be inspired by them in this respect can go a long way toward creating a meaningful connection with your audience that is already supported in Shakespeare's script.

When the principal comedian takes stage and makes their first impression on the audience, it's important to subtly establish two things:

1. the performer's ease; that the clown is genuinely comfortable experiencing vulnerability in front of an audience;
2. the importance of the audience; that the clown accepts and reacts to the presence and behavior of the audience in real-time.

When the audience feels that you're genuinely at ease within this initial exchange, a relationship of rapport can develop. Rapport between actor and audience feels harmonious, and in this relationship the audience can effortlessly empathize with the performer's feelings. The audience is at ease, but engaged, and they feel confident in the clown. They aren't worried about the performer or production.

We've all seen performances where we feel that the actor is uncomfortable, and, as a result, we, the audience, become uncomfortable as well. This is the case even if we're not immediately conscious of it. Ease and rapport with an audience is the opposite of that. When the audience trusts the clown, they can more freely invest in the action and even feel that they are in cahoots with the clown's thought process and antics. In short, they can find the performance funny.

Before we proceed, I need to acknowledge the impact of Avner Eisenberg and Julie Goell on the sensibilities and techniques that follow. I am deeply indebted to them both for teaching me at the Celebration Barn during the summers of 2001 and 2002. Learning from these two expert clowns and gifted teachers helped me better understand and develop my skills not only in the challenging and rewarding art of Clown, but also as an actor and artist. Avner Eisenberg was the first solo clown to appear on Broadway in his show *Avner the Eccentric*. He was the Jewel in the film *Jewel of the Nile*, and in 2002 he was inducted into the International Clown Hall of Fame. His wife, Julie Goell, trained in Commedia dell'arte, Mime, and Clown in Italy, and toured throughout Europe and later throughout the world. She appeared on Broadway in *Ghetto* and wrote and starred in two one-woman shows, *Woman in a Suitcase*, and *Opening Night Carmen: A Mopera*, both of which toured worldwide. She passed away in 2016. Avner and I have kept in touch over the years, and he continues to teach and perform worldwide. I enthusiastically recommend all his workshops.

TECHNIQUE

Avner taught me a technique for meeting the audience for the first time; I call it Avner's Technique and will describe it shortly. Learning the structure of this technique is an excellent starting place for meeting the audience and forging an effective bond with them. Avner's approach to clown is built on several core premises, one of which is: the audience was there first.

In the conventional theatre, the audience is typically seated before the actors take stage and the play begins. Let's begin by recognizing that the audience—from their perspective—was in the theatre before the clown. If an audience member arrived and took their seat twenty minutes before the clown takes stage, then that audience member feels like they were in the theatre first. This has a significant impact on this first encounter.

Just like you wouldn't barge into someone's apartment without first being invited in, the clown seeking to build an enjoyable relationship with their audience will not barge in:

the clown will ask to enter the stage. In his *Physical Comedy Handbook*, Davis Robinson describes this initial point of contact with the audience as similar to the sentence, "I am." We can add the element of genuine comfort to this statement and describe this contact as "I am comfortable with you watching me." It's a vulnerable yet secure place to begin bonding with your audience. We'll accomplish this ease through staging and, most importantly, breath.

STAGING

Let's assume you're performing on a proscenium stage. From offstage left, behind the proscenium arch, the clown peeks around the side and takes a step onto the stage while scanning the audience. The clown might be thinking something simple such as "You're there." This inner monologue is accompanied with an inhale. The clown receives confirmation from the audience that they're present and then brings their other foot onto the stage. The clown then releases the breath as if to say, "I know." The clown is now standing onstage in the "I am comfortable with you watching me."

This entrance has three moments and takes about two seconds. It establishes that the audience is important because during your scan you made contact with them. It also establishes that you're genuinely comfortable being open and vulnerable with them because you released your breath.

BREATHING IS IMPORTANT

Genuine ease gives the audience permission to enjoy the comedy. Another premise in Avner's approach is that when the breathing cycle is free—particularly with a release after the exhale at the bottom of the cycle—the audience will subconsciously interpret this behavior as a genuine sign of vulnerability, non-threat, and ease. This release is the letting go of that last bit of holding, that last bit of "fight, flight, or freeze" that we tend to subconsciously keep in reserve at the bottom of the exhale "just in case." The audience isn't conscious of the performer's breathing, but they begin to breathe in empathy all the same.

Breathing is an automatic function. This is why we can sleep and don't have to think about breathing twenty-four hours a day. Exertion and stress can influence this automatic function, and we can influence it with our thoughts as well.

An unselfconscious, free breathing cycle progresses something like this:

- impulse to breathe, followed by an inhale, then . . .
- a short moment of suspension, then . . .
- an impulse to release the breath, followed by an exhale, and then . . .
- a short moment of nothing at the bottom of the exhale, and then . . .
- the impulse to breathe again, followed by another inhale.

Hopefully this cycle continues for many years. But, joking aside, this is likely what you're doing when unselfconscious and simply reading this book or in other ways living your life. However, the anxiety of being in front of an audience can interfere with this cycle.

At the risk of oversimplifying: humans are herd animals. Similar to other herd animals, deep in our animal brain, there is a reflexive fear of being abandoned by the herd. When we separate ourselves from the herd like we do when performing, it can activate this fear. We can then begin to hold our breath as part of our fight, freeze, or flight defense response. Regardless of the cause, holding our breath only further fuels our anxiety. That anxiety will eventually be perceived by the audience at some level, even if unconsciously, and they begin to become concerned about the performer. Our release of the breath is the most vulnerable part of the breathing cycle because during that release we are not ready to immediately fight or flee. This release is deeply associated with ease and non-threat. So, if you notice that you're holding your breath, simply allow yourself to release in the next moment. The audience will tend to unconsciously adopt our breathing pattern.

CLOWN LOGIC

Clowns are logical problem-solvers—perhaps with absurd results but always with a logical process. In some ways, this is similar to the way children are rational problem-solvers. It's possible that you've seen and heard children say and do ridiculous but plausible things. As a parent, I saw my daughters regularly employ clown logic while growing up. Below are a couple of examples.

As a toddler, one of my daughters was walking and stepped on a Post-it note, which stuck to the bottom of her foot. She stopped walking, and, while still standing, bent down at the waist, and with both hands took hold of the paper. Without bending her leg at the knee, she then lifted her foot off the floor with both hands to inspect the Post-it note and promptly fell over. This entire sequence took about two seconds.

A few years later, she and her sister wanted to fill the backyard sky with bubbles. They became frustrated because no matter how fast they tried to blow bubbles, they couldn't produce enough of them. One saw the air pump laying on the driveway, and they quickly hatched a plan to put the bubble fluid into the air pump, thereby increasing their bubble-making capacity. It didn't work, but their clown logic was solid: more air should create more bubbles.

The clown-logic formula is simple and effective. Engage in a task, recognize a problem, find the problem interesting, discover a way to solve that problem. The effort to solve it either works or it creates a new problem. If the solution to the problem works, then release, and experience that satisfaction. If the solution doesn't work, then find the new problem interesting, and repeat the process until a solution is reached or there is an interruption. Here's a simple example:

- Clown sees some spilled coffee on an otherwise clean kitchen counter. (Recognize problem.)
- Clown finds problem interesting.
- Clown sees clean dishrag. (Discover solution.)
- Clown cleans up the coffee drips. (Solves problem. Release.)
- Clown sees that the otherwise clean dishrag now has coffee on it. (Recognizes new problem.)
- Clown sees glass of clean water. (Discovers solution.)
- Clown submerges coffee-stained dishrag into clean water and washes it. (Solves problem. Release.)
- Clown now sees that coffee stains have dirtied the water. (Recognizes new problem.)
- Clown finds problem interesting.
- Clown sees clean coffee maker. (Discovers solution.)
- Clown prepares coffee maker to filter the dirty water, puts clean coffee filter into the coffee maker, fills reservoir with the dirtied water, presses the brew button. (Solves problem.)
- Clown leans against the clean counter and enjoys their victory as the coffee maker runs its cycle. (Release. Experience satisfaction.)

In everyday life, we often try to solve problems as simply and efficiently as possible. Struggle, however, is dramatically interesting. Plausible, logical, and yet unusual complications help to create clown routines. How can I solve this everyday problem in an unconventional way?

EXPERIENCE AND SHARE

When we start bonding with our audience, we have to avoid a common acting trap: indicating. This trap applies to Clown and Shakespeare as much as it does to contemporary realism. It's useful to think of indicating in two ways: one that doesn't include the audience and one that does. Indicating is:

- indicating an experience, rather than having an experience (this is a trap for actors in all styles);
- demonstrating an idea to the audience rather than sharing an experience with them (this is seen in performances that don't have a fourth wall).

In most modern acting techniques, actors are taught to experience what is happening to them in the given circumstances rather than indicating what they think they should be feeling or what they think the audience should be seeing. Experiencing rather than indicating tends to make the acting more truthful and, as a result, more believable and compelling. Committing to this requires trust in oneself and trust that the audience is paying attention.

This applies to clowns as well. For example, to experience how good you feel in your new outfit is more truthful than showing the audience by mugging a happy facial expression and pointing insistently to your cufflinks. Experiencing the imaginary circumstances is always more truthful, detailed, and authentic than indicating, which tends to lead toward generalized clichés.

When trained actors indicate, they're often responding to a low level of desperation to impress their audience. This is outside of our definition of acting. Trying to impress an audience is different than trying to please an audience. You'll likely recognize this difference in your personal life: when was the last time someone genuinely pleased you by desperately trying to impress you? How did their over-effort make you feel? Desperation to impress is born out of insecurity and anxiety, and that's what the audience perceives when we indicate. Allow yourself to experience what is actually happening and trust that your genuine experience is sufficient for the audience to get it. The truth of the moment doesn't require or benefit from anything extra. If you find yourself indicating, gently nudge your attention back onto your genuine experience, your fellow actor, or the audience that exists in real-time, right now.

Clowns are comfortable with an audience, but it's problematic for actors or clowns to think of "showing" the audience anything. It's more useful to think of sharing with the audience, allowing them to simply witness what you are genuinely experiencing. I've found that when actors "show" something to the audience that it leads to indicating and the host of problems that brings. Showing requires effort; sharing requires an absence of effort. It's in that relative stillness that the audience is more likely to perceive the clown's thought process, actions, and emotional life. It's in those simple moments that the audience bonds with the clown.

BUILDING A LAUGH

Now that we've met the audience, let's strengthen this connection. For example, if the principal comedian is in a scene with another character and the audience laughs, the principal comedian is free to react to them and softly direct their attention toward them. This reenforces to the audience that they are important—that their behavior matters—and that the clown is comfortable being laughed at.

Share with the audience when it's useful. In live theatre, the moment that a clown should always share with the audience is the satisfaction of having solved a problem. Depending on the audience you can also share additional parts of your thought process. How much and when? Whatever pleases your audience. Clowns act for the pleasure of the audience.

Below is our earlier coffee example. I've added some potential moments of sharing noted within the parenthesis. I suggest you read this example twice and imagine the performance in two different ways: one where the clown shares their genuine experience described, and another where the clown shows a cliché-plagued, indicated concept of the experience described. Sometimes briefly experiencing how not to do something helps us better understand how to do something.

- Clown sees some spilled coffee on an otherwise clean kitchen counter. (Recognize problem, then . . .)
- Clown finds problem interesting.
- Clown sees clean dishrag. (Discover solution, then . . .)
- Clown cleans up the coffee drips. (Solves problem, release, shares satisfaction with the audience, then . . .)
- Clown sees that the otherwise clean dishrag now has coffee on it. (Recognizes new problem, then . . .)
- Clown sees glass of clean water. (Discovers solution, then . . .)

- Clown submerges coffee-stained dishrag into clean water and washes it. (Solves problem, release, shares satisfaction with the audience, then . . .)
- Clown now sees that coffee stains have dirtied the water in the glass. (Recognizes new problem, then . . .)
- Clown finds problem interesting.
- Clown sees clean coffee maker. (Discovers solution, then . . .)
- Clown prepares coffee maker to filter the dirty water, puts clean coffee filter into the coffee maker, fills reservoir with the dirtied water, presses start. (Solves problem, then . . .)
- Clown leans against the clean counter and enjoys their victory as the coffee maker runs its cycle. (Release. Experience satisfaction. Share satisfaction with audience.)

Please note how specific these moments are. Sanford Meisner said, "good acting is specific." Good Clown is too.

INVITE RATHER THAN INSIST

It's interesting that when an audience notices an actor is trying to be funny, they resist laughing. This puts practitioners in a challenging situation: we want the audience to laugh, but if they can tell that we're trying to make them laugh, then they don't want to laugh. Most people just don't like feeling forced to do something.

The audience didn't come to the theatre to fake an emotional experience. They want to have whatever experience they feel like having rather than feeling obliged to perform a reaction for the clown or cast. Modern practitioners should accept this and welcome the audience to have their unique experience of the play. We want to invite the audience to experience the humor in the performance while not insisting that they must laugh.

The clown's costume helps to set this tone, and it's an important part of the principal comedian's total image which we'll discuss shortly. The costume should be plausibly unusual and visually distinctive while not appearing unreasonably silly or surprisingly mundane. It should invite the audience to enjoy themselves but not insist that they find the costume amusing.

When working with your costume designer on a principal comedian role in Shakespeare's comedies, ask yourself: Does this costume invite your audience to laugh? Does it invite your audience to laugh while still being plausible in the world of the play? The director should work with the costume designer to set the clown up for success. It's nice if the clown can have a say in the design as well. What will help them develop an effective relationship with the audience?

The costume fuses with the character's face, hair, body, and important hand props to create a total image. This is the character's "look," everything that the audience can see related to that character. Together they can stimulate the audience's imagination and have an impact similar to a theatrical mask. For example, the red nose of the circus clown invites the audience to not take the character too seriously. Its shape suggests the roundness of a toddler's face. The red color suggests intoxication. We associate both of these with impulsiveness and less inhibited behavior. This small mask invites the audience to expect humor.

It's helpful for the actor to become comfortable with allowing the total image to play because it makes an impression on the audience's collective mind. When meeting the audience for the first time, after the moment of "I am comfortable with you watching me," allow the "look" to impact the audience. Breathe easy as you scan the audience, kind of like saying, "I know I look like this." This only takes a couple seconds, but it helps the audience bond with the performer from the beginning. This level of simplicity can feel a little scary. It can feel vulnerable, and anxieties such as "I'm not doing anything" can emerge for both actor and director. It requires some bravery.

Some of the techniques we use when acting in the theatrical masks of the Commedia dell'arte can apply to the total image as well. These masks possess extreme facial features. When designed thoughtfully and used skillfully they can intrigue the audience and invite them to expect humor and laughter. But before we proceed with those techniques, let's take a brief tangent into Commedia mask design. Though not directly connected with the subject of this book, I hope this brief tangent can help us better understand the difference between inviting and insisting.

CAPITANO MASK TANGENT

A helpful example for understanding the difference between inviting and insisting is the Capitano mask. This mask traditionally has phallic qualities, with the long nose alluding to the length of an erect penis and the nostrils of the mask suggesting testicles. A question mask designers need to ask themselves is: how closely should the nose resemble an actual penis?

Some mask-makers allow the long nose to remain an abstract suggestion of a penis. This choice invites the audience to use their imaginations, to make the connection themselves and fill in the details. In this way, the audience becomes complicit with the mask's impact on them. If they start to view the mask as sexual, they're part of that process and have to accept responsibility for their part of it. Their imagination has made them complicit in the obscenity. The mask invited them to do that.

This is in contrast to the Capitano masks where the designer has opted for a more literal depiction of a penis. This mask doesn't require the audience to use their imaginations. It doesn't invite the audience to become complicit. It just tells them what to think. These masks can feel insistent, like the mask is trying to force the viewer to laugh at an actual penis on a person's face. In my experience, it's usually better to invite than insist, in both performance and mask design.

CAMEO

When I studied Commedia with the Dell'Arte players in 2001, they taught us a technique they referred to as a "cameo." Essentially, it's a way to present the mask just after entering the stage and also just before leaving the stage. Performing this cameo helps the mask, actor, and character's total image make both an initial and final impact on the audience. It helps to establish the relationship with the audience in the beginning of a scene and strengthen it just prior to leaving the stage.

For our purposes, this technique is most useful just prior to exiting the stage. (Avner's Technique helps establish our initial relationship with the audience.) The technique is simple. Towards the end of the scene, the clown crosses to the exit point, turns, and looks into the space one last time. While looking into the space, the performer might speak their final line to another character, or speak it to their audience, or share their nonverbal satisfaction with the audience, or do some other thing that makes an impression. They then turn and exit the stage.

Presenting a cameo just before leaving the stage strengthens a clown's bond with the audience. Other characters can perform cameos too. You can even see cameos in multi-camera sitcoms when a character will walk to the door, turn back into the space to deliver a line or gesture, and then walk through the door and off camera. Performing a cameo allows the character's image to make one last impression on the audience before their exit. In comedy, presenting a cameo makes an impact. It helps the audience look forward to your character's return to the stage.

SIGNATURE GESTURES

In addition to allowing their total image to "play," clowns and comedians can also develop signature gestures and phrases for their characters. These gestures aren't mandatory parts of the performance, but they can be very useful tools. Once established, they give the audience something to look forward to and invite them to laugh.

For example, one of Bill Hader's characters from *Saturday Night Live*, Stefon, employs the signature phrase of "It has everything." He uses it in each sketch, and the audience loves it when he says it. Hader also has a signature gesture for Stefon where he covers his mouth with his hands and looks straight ahead. In *Sanford and Son*, Redd Foxx's Fred Sanford would put one hand over his heart and extend the other one toward the sky faking a heart attack when events weren't going his way. During this gesture he often cried out to his deceased wife, Elizabeth, that he was "comin' to join you, honey." This signature phrase and gesture for Redd Foxx's Fred Sanford was so beloved that it appeared in Eddie Murphy's performance in *Shrek 2* more than twenty years later when Donkey shouts out, "I'm comin' Elizabeth," just before succumbing to the magic potion.

Both Foxx and Hader used signature gestures and phrases to punctuate important moments for their characters, and to please their audiences. For Shakespeare's comedies, we'll focus on developing signature gestures since the words have already been provided by the playwright.

DEVELOPING SIGNATURE GESTURES

To develop a signature gesture, experiment with physical gestures that are simple, safely repeatable, only take a second or two to complete, and are in some way unusual or extreme. You don't want to choose anything that is too elaborate or would put the actor at risk of injury. Set a timer for five minutes, and, while working on your feet, experiment and accumulate about six options. Keep working even if you periodically feel blocked. It's when you feel out of ideas that you're actually in a productive space to surprise yourself with startling authenticity. In rehearsal, a place of "not knowing" can become a very creative space when we embrace it. Once you have five minutes' worth of gesture options, share your favorite gestures with your director or classmates. A couple will eventually emerge as your favorites. You want to find signature gestures that are both enjoyable for you to perform and that also resonate with your audience and director.

Avner uses the idea of a touchdown dance to inspire signature gestures. Pretend to catch the ball (or catch a real ball if you like) and then do a touchdown dance. Do this a few times. Notice the options people respond to. Also notice which options feel natural for you to perform. Another version of this exercise is to miss or drop the ball in the end zone and then do the same touchdown dance of celebration. One or two gestures will emerge as favorites.

USING SIGNATURE GESTURES

Signature gestures are useful for punctuating important moments and can be used at any time. They can be employed when the character is experiencing a victory or a defeat. They can also be used as part of a character's preparation for an event, such as preparing to confront one's boss about low wages. The character might rehearse their words, gestures, and overall staging, and, once thoroughly prepared to confront their boss, perform the signature gesture. Signature gestures can also be used just after presenting a cameo at one's exit to help strengthen that last impression on an audience at the end of a scene.

In the television series *Happy Days*, the character Fonzie would put his thumbs up when he experienced satisfaction with his hair or a situation. This signature gesture was very effective and part of what made Fonzie one of the most memorable characters of that series.

CAPITALIZING ON RELATIONSHIPS

Though not always stated this way, most modern acting techniques teach us to identify, craft, and embody relationships. When we deliberately serve the play by using our imaginations to create an emotionally significant, imaginary point of view on a person or object, we're crafting a relationship. When we endow an object or a person with a history and emotionally significant qualities, we are crafting a relationship. In a scene when your character treats their sibling differently than their lover, the actor is articulating the differences in those two relationships. Same with objects; when we treat jewelry given to us by our lover differently than jewelry given from a sibling, we are articulating relationship.

Clowns also have relationships with people and objects, and we can capitalize on the acting techniques you already know to develop them. The exercises below adapt the skills many practitioners already have by putting your attention on the areas most useful for principal comedian roles in Shakespeare's comedies.

RELATIONSHIP TO COSTUME

We've already learned that Shakespeare's audience could recognize the principal comedian in a play based on their costume. That their unique costume was part of the total image that invited that audience to laugh. Building a relationship to costume can be very useful for the modern practitioner in Shakespeare's comedies. Does your character talk about or reference their clothes?

You'll recall that Elizabethan society was quite rigid and stratified by contemporary standards. One's garments helped people understand that person's status in that society and how they should be treated as a result. This is one of the reasons that certain colors and fabrics were reserved exclusively for the nobility. Changing one's clothes in a Shakespeare play is not as casual as it might be in a contemporary play. Does your character change costume?

In contemporary clown, as we've already discussed, the costume gives the audience permission to laugh. The fool's motley, the countryside outfit, the too-small form-fitting rocker shirt that exposes the belly; these can invite the audience to laugh. The costume plants in the audience's mind the expectation that this character will be funny, and they then begin to expect certain behaviors from that character as a result. Sometimes the costume is a sight gag, a joke in its own right.

The costume can also provoke the clown to experience how their costume makes them feel. You've likely experienced this yourself when you feel confident while being well dressed and the opposite when being dressed poorly. We can also see this in more extreme ways with younger children who feel particularly special wearing sparkly princess shoes, cowboy boots, and other favorite clothes. Most children aren't trying to indicate how they feel about their outfits; they simply feel their feelings in an unselfconscious way and share them. Those feelings are then perceived by their audience.

STATUS AND COSTUME

Children are also good examples of a person experiencing the status that their clothing brings them. Is it the special dress or cowboy boots causing the child to feel so proud? In *A Christmas Story*, the pink Easter Bunny outfit makes Ralphie feel embarrassed; it lowers his status. If your character changes costume, how does their status change? How do they feel about their new status?

EXERCISE: RELATIONSHIP TO COSTUME

To prepare for this exercise, add one special costume item to your normal acting-studio wardrobe. This might be a jacket, scarf, hat, ribbon, shoes, or something else that is distinct and feels special.

INSTRUCTIONS
- Make a simple entrance. ("I am comfortable being watched.")
- Experience how the costume makes you feel. ("I am wearing these clothes.")
- Breathe easy. (Allow total image to play.)
- Share your experience without indicating.
- Perform signature gesture if you have the impulse to do so.

- When you have the impulse to exit, then cross to the exit point.
- Present a cameo and then exit the stage.

How did you feel about your special costume piece in the exercise? How did it change your status? If you were performing in front of a classroom audience, how did their reaction (or lack of reaction) change your status?

In these exercises, it's important to be specific and clear. Allow each moment to be its own action. If you find that you're blending moments together, ask yourself if you're rushing due to anxiety or is it something else. Help yourself if you can, then exhale and do the exercise again. Specific actions create clarity for the audience. One action at a time. Dare to take as much time as necessary.

Also, if you catch yourself indicating, put your attention back onto experiencing what's happening and continue breathing. Just like good contemporary acting, experiencing the pride, embarrassment, or other feeling that comes with the special costume piece is enough. Showing is not necessary or helpful.

ADVANCED VERSIONS

- Make an entrance in your everyday acting studio clothes and bring the special costume piece with you. Once you take stage as explained earlier, put that special costume piece on in front of the audience. Share your experience with the audience. Does adding the special piece to your costume raise or lower your status? When you have the impulse to exit, then exit.
- Begin as described above, but, after you put the special costume piece on, share something cool your costume

can do with your audience. Do the zippers, snaps, or Velcro make interesting sounds? Does the special costume piece shine? Can you do tricks with the drawstrings? Can your costume piece change your appearance? How does this, and the audience's reaction to it, change your status? Keep your attention on experiencing how these actions make you feel. Keep breathing and accept the audience's response. React if you have the impulse to do so. When you have the impulse to exit, then exit.

RELATIONSHIP TO PROP

Similar to the section on costume above, clowns can also build relationships with props. Just like characters in conventional plays build relationships with objects—this baseball glove was given to me by my father, this piece of pottery was thrown by my mother, etc.—it's also useful for clowns, particularly the principal comedian.

We've already mentioned the bauble used by the professional fool. In addition to being a play sword, scepter, or phallic symbol, the bauble is also part of the fool's total visual image. It's one of the items that gives the fool permission to periodically step outside of the status hierarchy and speak truth to power or even usurp the play's narrative.

But in Shakespeare's comedies, useful relationships to props aren't restricted to just a bauble. There are many places to explore here and many places to craft significant relationships to objects. Our everyday life can be useful inspiration. Gifts, souvenirs, heirlooms, good bargains, or exceptional finds at the secondhand music store can all become important objects in our lives. What might your clown's equivalent be? Children can build significant relationships and become enthralled with simple items such as blankets, sticks, rocks, or a cardboard box. What appeals to your clown? Don Armado speaks of his sword; Malvolio has a strong relationship with the letter he finds. Though not a stage clown, Rosalind has a strong relationship with a poem she finds on a palm tree. What opportunities exist for the role you're working on?

EXERCISE: RELATIONSHIP TO PROP

This exercise follows the same format as the costume exercise you did earlier. In addition to your normal acting studio wardrobe, add one special hand prop. This might be a bauble, a hand mirror, a sword, a staff, a musical instrument, or something else.

Now—as earlier in the costume exercise—make a simple entrance, take stage, hold stage allowing the prop to be seen by the audience, experience and share how the prop makes you feel and changes your status, signature gesture if you have the impulse to do so, and when you have the impulse to exit, exit. Perform a cameo if you have the impulse to do so.

ADVANCED VERSION

Make a simple entrance and hold stage as before, allowing the prop to be seen by the audience as you experience how the prop makes you feel. When you have the impulse to do so, show us one cool thing you can do with your prop. Keep breathing and accept however the audience responds. Does their reaction raise or lower your status? What does their reaction make you want to do? React if you have the impulse to do so. If you're not sure, just breathe. Signature gesture if you have that impulse. When you have the impulse to exit, cross to the exit point, cameo, and then exit.

PUTTING IT TOGETHER

Let's see how some of the elements we've explored in this chapter might come together in a performance. For this example, we'll look at Pompey in Shakespeare's *Measure for Measure*. Pompey was probably played by the principal comedian Robert Armin.

Pompey is a pimp, and he finds himself in prison midway through the play. He's been offered a reduced sentence if he assists the executioner, Abhorson, with a couple of beheadings. Pompey agrees, and in Act 4, scene 3, he sets the axe and chopping block on the stage before addressing the audience with his longest speech in the play.

My inspiration and justification for having Pompey set the axe and chopping block at the top of this scene is that this play was performed in universal lighting without the blackout conventions we have now. The axe and block had to get on the stage in plain sight of the audience. How might this set-up become entertaining? Below is a description of some possible actions.

EXAMPLE: POMPEY IN MEASURE FOR MEASURE

On a nearly bare stage, Pompey enters from stage right using the entrance technique we explained earlier. Though this is not the first time the audience has met Pompey in the play, it's the first time the audience is alone with him. It's justified to strengthen that bond at the top of the scene.

In keeping with his new position as executioner's helper, Pompey is wearing a patched-together, homemade, executioner's hood—an important part of an executioner's uniform. Pompey allows the costume to play with the audience in the "I am wearing this hood" moment. This invites the audience to laugh and also communicates a change of occupation and status for Pompey the pimp.

As Pompey surveys the audience, he discovers that the stage is bare and that the executioner's block is not on stage. He recognizes a problem. He looks around for the chopping block and discovers it offstage. He discovers a solution. He shares his discovery and relief with the audience and then exits the stage. The stage is empty for a brief moment.

Then Pompey returns, straining with all his might to carry a very large chopping block. He is attempting to solve the problem. With great effort, he's able to place the block in the correct position. He solves the problem. Release. He shares his satisfaction at a job well done with the audience, letting them know they matter. This success raises Pompey's status.

Pompey then discovers that the block is missing its axe. Recognizing this new problem lowers his status. He quickly surveys the room again—which doesn't take as long since he just surveyed it a minute ago. He discovers the axe offstage. Inner monologue of "duh!" as he exits in that direction. The stage is again empty for a brief moment.

Pompey returns to stage again, this time ass first, straining to drag a very large executioner's axe behind him. As he attempts to solve the problem, he's presenting a change of image by entering ass first. This change is justified by an earlier scene when a character refers to Pompey's large "bum." Staying as far away from the blade as possible because he doesn't want to get cut, and with great effort, Pompey places the axe upon the chopping block. He's solved the problem with clown logic.

Pompey experiences a sense of satisfaction from his success. His status rises. He has the impulse to stand on the block and pose for the audience. He then experiences his victory anew, performs his signature gesture, and releases. He descends from the chopping block and scans the audience. He then has the impulse to speak the first line of his monologue.

This entire sequence has taken less than two minutes, and has gained credit with the audience so that the actor is in a confident, credible position to deliver a challenging speech.

At the conclusion of the monologue, the executioner, Abhorson, enters. He's a real-deal executioner with a menacing costume and demeanor. Pompey's status lowers as a result. Pompey shares his intimidation with the audience, strengthening that bond. We are now fully in a conventional scene.

KEY TAKEAWAYS

- Contemporary clown techniques and sensibilities can help us better realize and inhabit Shakespeare's comedic design.
- The principal comedian's function is to bridge the everyday world of the audience and the imaginary world of Shakespeare's play with humor and empathy.
- Clowns are logical problem-solvers.
- Clowns are in direct contact with their audience. There isn't a fourth wall.
- When meeting the audience for the first time, the clown needs to establish the importance of the audience and that the clown is genuinely comfortable onstage.
- Signature gestures are useful for the clown.
- Status changes are interesting and can be shared with the audience.
- Costume can be a useful invitation for the audience to laugh. Allow the total image to play.
- Cameos can strengthen the bond with the audience.
- Modern practitioners can adapt and capitalize on the techniques they already possess to build effective relationships with costumes and props.
- Just as in realism, it's better for the clown to experience what is happening than indicate how they are feeling.

TRAPS AND PITFALLS
FEARFUL THINKING
Meeting the audience can feel vulnerable because it is. Just like acting any role, it's more useful to stay in character and think the thoughts of the clown rather than think unproductively. As you practice and gain experience, you'll become more comfortable with this level of public vulnerability. Be patient with yourself, but seek to become confident with feeling vulnerable.

NOT RELATING WITH YOUR AUDIENCE
Are you engaging and relating with your audience, just looking at them, or not even really looking at them? Many contemporary acting techniques teach us to look just over the audience's heads or at the railing of the balcony or something like that. Scan your actual audience and pay attention to them. Relate with all of them, not just the folks center in row A but the folks far left in row M and the folks far right in row Z. You want them all to feel like they matter.

PUSHY INSISTENCE
It's not useful to become pushy or insistent. Insistency is when the performer tries to force the audience to have a certain emotional experience, like trying to force the audience to laugh, for example. It's a behavior that's born out of fear and unmet expectations, and it can make the clown appear insecure or annoyed. Pushy insistence feels like the clown is trying to force their way into the apartment rather than asking to be invited in. It can damage the bond you're trying to establish with your audience. It's usually more effective to simply accept the audience's experience of the performance, listen to their resultant behavior, and then react to that. Stay truthful in your relationship with the audience.

AUDIBLE BREATHING

Are your inhales and exhales making sounds when you enter? If yes, then ask yourself: Am I freely breathing or am I showing the audience that I am breathing? Audible breathing can be distracting and usually reads as untruthful to an audience. It's important to breathe because it communicates comfort and ease, but there's no need to demonstrate or prove to anyone that you are breathing.

RUSHING

Are you in a hurry onstage? Just like when acting realism, it's important to experience the impulse to do an action before doing the action. This way, the action is justified and believable. When we hurry as a result of actor anxiety, we tend to lose clarity and believability. Allow each moment to take as much time as necessary; no more and no less.

CROWDING THE AUDIENCE

When first learning to clown, it's a common mistake to crowd the audience. It usually comes from a desire to bond with them by closing the distance between you. The problem with that strategy is that it looks and feels pushy. When we crowd the audience, it's like we've been invited into their apartment and then proceed to suddenly do that too-close talking thing. It's usually off-putting. In your initial encounter with the audience, where's the distance that feels comfortable—not pushy and also not standoffish? Experiment. Notice the impact different distances have on your audience.

TRYING TO BE INTERESTING

I've heard a couple people say this over the years, but Avner was the first: "go onstage to get interested, not to be interesting." It's a very useful and brilliantly concise direction.

Allow yourself to get interested in the audience, your costume, or the problem you're trying to solve. When we try to be interesting, we're actually trying to impress an audience and we lose touch with the truth of the moment. If you notice yourself doing that, simply put your attention back onto the audience, the other character, or what you're doing, and choose to get involved with that.

Language

Clarity, Variety, and Humor

Five

INTRODUCTION

Most of the books on acting Shakespeare focus on his language. Though this book doesn't focus on heightened language to the extent that many excellent books do, it would be an omission not to address it in some form. Working effectively with Shakespeare's language is a very important concern for modern practitioners. This chapter presents concepts and lessons I've found to be most helpful when working on Shakespeare's comedies, their language, and the desired impact on the audience. These lessons assume that the practitioners appreciate the importance of clearly comprehending the dialogue. If the artists involved in creating the production don't understand the play, it's very unlikely that an audience will either.

Unfortunately, many audience members expect to be confused when attending a Shakespeare play. Increasingly, audiences in the USA are not already familiar with the general narratives of even Shakespeare's most recognized works. This makes our responsibility even greater. The modern practitioner needs to tell the story clearly, believably, and with a high level of entertainment value or else risk confirming the audience's suspicions that the play will be confusing or boring. In this chapter, we'll learn how to communicate a clear and varied narrative that realizes Shakespeare's comedic design and entertains today's audience.

DOI: 10.4324/9781003273967-5

KEY LESSONS: CLARITY, VARIETY, HUMOR

Clarity, variety, and humor are important when crafting a compelling performance or production. These three concerns will guide us through this key lesson on identifying and utilizing the comedic opportunities in Shakespeare's language. As already discussed, clarity is necessary for an audience to become enthralled in the story. We'll then explore variety, which is dramatically dynamic, lifelike, creates opportunities for surprises, and, as a result, keeps the audience involved. Predictability, on the other hand, is usually not dramatically useful because it creates a situation where the audience no longer needs to listen, and that can be a huge problem in a heightened language play. Lastly, we'll learn to recognize opportunities for humor in Shakespeare's language and how we can utilize those opportunities while keeping the action plausible for a modern audience.

A PUNCTUATION PREAMBLE

We will continue to use the punctuation from Shakespeare's first folio, updated with contemporary spelling and capitalization in this chapter. When comparing punctuation in the different editions of Shakespeare, it's helpful to keep one's attention on the creative process and less on trying to establish any kind of absolute correctness. It's impossible to know with certainty what punctuation Shakespeare actually wrote because many of his plays were not published until after his death. Even prior to his death, printers of the day were known to take liberties. Also, what was considered correct spelling and grammar was not as defined as it is today. In my own creative work, I use first folio punctuation unless there is a compelling reason not to use it, such as missing dialogue, or if the first folio punctuation confuses the practitioners more than it illuminates.

Which version should you use in your work? Use the version that appeals to you given the role or production you're working on. Our ongoing desire to please our audience is usually more important than abiding by any "correct" version of the script. The audience wants to experience an entertaining story and is usually much less interested in what edition of the script is being used.

When grappling with a particularly challenging section of language, it can be instructive to see how the punctuation in Shakespeare's first folio is similar and different from the punctuation in other versions. Punctuation can be a very important tool because it's one way many playwrights try to communicate with the practitioners. This was likely the case with Shakespeare given the abbreviated timeline they had for rehearsals. But, unfortunately, we cannot know for sure what punctuation he intended.

CHOOSING AND EMPHASIZING

We'll use the terms "choose" and "emphasize" throughout this chapter. To "choose" is a technique whereby the actor has the character reject other options before completing their thought. To choose a word is similar to ordering a drink from a menu: the character sees the three choices and rejects cola and lemon-lime before choosing root beer. "I'll have the fish tacos [short moment of choosing] and a root beer." The time it takes to choose is typically the speed of thought: how long it takes the actor to think the thoughts about the rejected options. "I'll have the fish tacos and [not cola, not lemon-lime, yes] a root beer."

To emphasize is when the actor places importance on a word or phrase by changing the pitch, the volume, the stress, or the pace of their talking. "I'll have the FISH tacos and a root beer" is a volume example. Or you can combine emphasizing with choosing: "I'll have the FISH tacos and [let's see; no, no, ah] a root beer."

Choosing and emphasizing are simple, useful techniques you can apply with heightened language. Like all of the techniques in this book, however, they must be justified in order to be perceived as believable. Technique without justification is never quite believable, often boring, and never as compelling as it could become with justification. Choosing and emphasizing are not interesting in their own right; they are both ways that the character is trying to communicate in order to get their needs met.

CLARITY

Know what you're saying and why you're saying it, and then communicate that understanding to the other characters and your audience. This is the case in all plays and genres, but it's critical in comedy. If the audience doesn't perceive the joke, they cannot possibly respond with their laughter.

LENGTH OF THOUGHT: USING FULL STOPS

Look at your script and begin by identifying the number of thoughts your character speaks. Notice the length of those thoughts as well. We'll do this by noting the full stops in the script. Full stops are the periods, exclamation marks, and question marks within a speech and role.

Keeping the thoughts distinct from one another helps to make the speech clear. When a character speaks a new thought, they will almost always play a new action. In this context, the term "action" means the verb the actor is playing on the line in an effort to get their character's needs met or to achieve an objective that exists in the other character's behavior. Charm, threaten, intrigue, scare, and lure are all examples of playable actions. It's a good idea to think of a new thought as an obligation to change your action because it will make the performance more specific. Sometimes it's possible to play more than one action within a complicated thought, but, at minimum, a new thought usually requires a new action.

Below are two speeches that we will reference regularly in this chapter. The first is Berowne from *Love's Labour's Lost* and the second is Portia from *The Merchant of Venice*. I've noted the word immediately before each full stop in bold so you can more easily see the number and lengths of the thoughts.

O, and I forsooth in love,
I that have been love's **whip**?
A very beadle to a humorous sigh: a critic,
Nay, a night-watch **constable**.
A domineering pedant ore the boy,
Then whom no mortal so magnificent,
This wimpled, whining, purblind wayward boy,
This signior Junios giant dwarf, don Cupid,
Regent of love-rimes, lord of folded arms,
Th' anointed sovereign of sighs and groans:
Liege of all loiterers and malcontents:
Dread prince of placates, king of **codpieces**.
Sole Imperator and great general
Of trotting paroters (o my little **heart**.)
And I to be a corporal of his field,
And wear his colors like a tumbler's **hoop**.
What? I love, I sue, I seek a wife,
A woman that is like a German clock,
Still a repairing: ever out of frame,
And never going a right, being a watch:

> But being watched, that it may still go **right**.
> Nay, to be perjured, which is worst of all:
> And among three, to love the worst of all,
> A whitely wanton, with a velvet **brow**.
> With two pitch balls stuck in her face for **eyes**.
> Aye, and by heaven, one that will do the deed,
> Though Argus were her eunuch and her **guard**.
> And I to sigh for her, to watch for her,
> To pray for her, go to: it is a plague
> That Cupid will impose for my neglect,
> Of his almighty dreadful little **might**.
> Well, I will love, write, sigh, pray, sue, groan,
> Some men must love my lady, and some **Joan**.

Berowne's speech has twelve thoughts. Note that some of the thoughts are quite long and some as short as one word. Let's look at Portia's speech.

> In terms of choice I am not solely led
> By nice direction of a maiden's eyes:
> Besides, the lottery of my destiny
> Bars me the right of voluntary choosing:
> But if my father had not scanted me,
> And hedged me by his wit to yield myself
> His wife, who wins me by that means I told you,
> Yourself (renowned prince) then stood as fair
> As any comer I have looked on yet
> For my **affection**.

Portia's speech is one thought. Length of thought is an important key into a character's emotional condition. When the thought changes, the actor should change. A speech with eleven thoughts will have very different rhythms than a speech consisting of only one thought. A character speaking one long complicated thought is having a very different experience than a character speaking eight short thoughts one after the other. They should be acted differently. That's part of Shakespeare's design.

EXERCISE: FULL STOP WALK

A simple and effective exercise to start embodying a speech is a version of the punctuation walk exercise; we'll explain the full exercise later in this chapter. For now, we'll only focus on full stops. Working on a speech with multiple thoughts such as Berowne's from above, walk in one direction as you speak until you come to a full stop. When you reach the full stop, change direction as you speak and play a different action. It's a surprisingly effective way to start embodying the changes within a speech.

SIMPLE THOUGHTS AND COMPLEX THOUGHTS

Simple thoughts should sound simple and to the point; complicated thoughts should sound more, well, complicated. "I'd like a glass of water," is a simple thought. The line communicates clearly when spoken simply. To speak that line as if it were complicated could confuse the listener.

When working on a complicated thought, it's useful to ask yourself: Why are these words necessary right now? Why not a simpler version? Why does the character or this play need these extra words? Are they needed to move the story, develop the character, or are they simply there for entertainment value? The line "Bring forth a vessel of clear, cold, aqua" is more complicated than "I'd like a glass of water," and the practitioners should ask themselves: Why these words right now? In this example, what do those additional words reveal about the character?

Below is one of Berowne's shorter, but still complicated, thoughts.

> And I to be a corporal of his field,
> And wear his colors like a tumbler's hoop.

In its simplest form, this thought means something close to "I feel weak and silly." That simple thought is all that's necessary to move the story. Why does Berowne and the play need Shakespeare's extra words right now? It's not just because it's a Shakespeare play. A "corporal" is a low-ranking soldier; this would make Cupid the General ordering Berowne around with little agency of his own. The "colors" of a battlefield are something like the flag of a nation. When Berowne says that he wears Cupid's colors "like a tumbler's hoop," he is casting himself as both loyal to Cupid (wearing his colors, showing his allegiance), but wearing them like a tumbler's hoop means to wear them like a court jester, who was associated with acrobatic tricks through a ribboned hoop. It ultimately creates quite the image with Berowne, a nobleman, becoming a low-ranking soldier in Cupid's battlefield with little agency of his own, simply wearing his allegiance like a fool uses a hoop.

Your own justification for Berowne's, or any character's, choice of words forges the path for your character development. It also lays out possibilities for other kinds of entertainment value while advancing the story's themes and director's point of view.

MOVING THE THOUGHT FORWARD

Upward inflection is important when speaking longer, more complicated thoughts. Upward inflection communicates to the listener that you have more to say, whereas downward inflection lets the listener know that you are finishing your thought. Downward inflection is problematic when it dominates our verse speaking. Habitual downward inflection has the effect of making a single complicated thought sound like a series of shorter thoughts, and that can be confusing to the listener. Turning longer thoughts into shorter thoughts through downward inflection can also make the speech more predictable and therefore less interesting. A character with more thoughts is experiencing their situation differently than a person with fewer thoughts.

Take a look at Berowne's response to his simple question.

> What? I love, I sue, I seek a wife,
> A woman that is like a German clock,
> Still a repairing: ever out of frame,
> And never going a right, being a watch:
> But being watched, that it may still go right.

His complicated response to his simple question or realization—"What?"—is an important acting direction for the modern practitioner. If we were to chop his response into smaller bits by treating most of the commas and all of the colons as full stops, it changes the speech dramatically. Go ahead and read this through aloud downward inflecting at each period.

> What? I love. I sue. I seek a wife.
> A woman that is like a German clock.
> Still a repairing. Ever out of frame.
> And never going a right, being a watch.
> But being watched. That it may still go right.

When we over end-stop and downward infect, we lose the arch of Berowne's passion, and the character starts to sound overly controlled or uninterested, perhaps even depressed. It's also likely that the joke in the last two lines doesn't play as well.

The ability to upward inflect until landing at a full stop is a useful skill, and it takes practice. This should not be confused with the North American Southern California Uptalk dialect that came into vogue during the 1980s and is still used throughout the English-speaking world. Upward inflection in our case is not perpetually asking questions; it's maintaining the character's desire to communicate by lifting up and forward until landing at the conclusion of the thought.

EXERCISE: UPWARD INFLECTION

A simple and effective exercise for developing this skill is to simply add the word "and" to the end of each line that does not end with a full stop.

> What? I love, I sue, I seek a wife, AND
> A woman that is like a German clock, AND
> Still a repairing: ever out of frame, AND
> And never going a right, being a watch: AND
> But being watched, that it may still go right. FULL STOP

Of course, the "and" is a rehearsal tool and isn't spoken during the actual performance. But this exercise will help you learn to keep the spoken thought moving forward until reaching a full stop. Having to speak the "and" without downward inflecting trains us to have both the breath reserve necessary to keep our inflection up and also the idea that we have more to say. Having more to say justifies keeping the thought moving forward.

VERSE

Verse follows a particular rhythm, and Shakespeare's predominant verse form is blank verse also known as unrhymed iambic pentameter. This is a ten-syllable line with five stressed syllables and five unstressed syllables. He also frequently writes feminine endings that include an extra unstressed syllable at the end of the verse line making the line eleven syllables. You can identify verse quickly on the page because each line begins with a capitalized word. The earlier Berowne and Portia speeches are both written in verse. It's useful for practitioners to view verse as a more intense expression than our everyday use of language. If our everyday speech were coffee, then verse would be espresso.

We have to address the issue of stress and meter briefly to avoid a stumbling block for well-intentioned practitioners. In iambic pentameter, stress is relative to the unstressed syllable in the same foot. Stressed syllables are not all spoken with the same level of emphasis. One syllable simply requires more stress than the other syllable in that two-syllable foot. We want to use the verse but avoid sounding robotic or in other ways unnatural. Let's revisit Berowne for a moment. The stressed syllables are in bold.

Of **his** / al**might**/y **dread**/ful **litt**/le **might**.

This is a ten-syllable line of iambic pentameter, but just because the words "his" and "might" are both stressed does not mean they're equally important. "Might" is much more important to the clarity and acting of the line than "his." "His" is only stressed relative to the "of." In fact, "his" may even be less emphasized than the following unstressed syllable "al-". Practitioners can still embrace the rhythm of iambic pentameter and sound very believable by not forcing syllables to have equal stress. That will tend to sound mechanical.

PROSE

In prose, each thought follows typical sentence structure, and the lines do not conform to a regular meter like we hear in blank verse. When Shakespeare uses prose, he is choosing a freer and more accessible structure. That structure can inform our choices.

When a character speaks prose, ask yourself, "Does Shakespeare intend this character to be funny?" It's not always the case, but it's important to ask the question. It's generally accepted that one reason Shakespeare wrote prose was to allow performance flexibility. This way, the actors could pause, improvise, or possibly even step out of the narrative entirely without the scene being bound to a particular rhythm. This latitude is particularly useful for a principal comedian trying to bond with their audience.

A shift into prose from verse is significant direction from the writer for the contemporary actor and director. A production that handles verse and prose identically is missing an opportunity for performance variety and for a change in overall dynamics within the story. *Twelfth Night* and *A Midsummer Night's Dream* are clear examples of this.

On the page, prose looks a lot like conventional writing. The lines don't always begin with a capitalized word. Here's a short excerpt from a speech by Launce in *The Two Gentlemen of Verona*:

> She hath more qualities than a water spaniel, which is
> much in a bare Christian: Here is the cate-log of her condition.

Prose can be a useful tool and dramatic shift within a verse-dominant play. But sometimes prose is the dominant form of expression in the play and not just a tool. This is the case in in *Much Ado about Nothing* and *The Merry Wives of Windsor*. Prose can bring us surprising levels of freedom within Shakespeare's comedic design. It's important not to dismiss it just because it doesn't follow a regular meter. We'll look at Launce more closely later in this book.

IF-THEN STRUCTURE: QUESTIONS AND ANSWERS

Questions should sound like questions. This usually requires upward inflection. It's confusing when a question sounds like a statement and vice versa. "Can I have a glass of water?" has a totally different impact when spoken like a statement. One's a request; the other sounds more aggressive.

One of the ways Shakespeare builds question-and-answer into his writing is with different manifestations of if-then statements. Like most questions, if-then rhetoric has a pitch pattern associated with it, where the if inflects up like asking a question, and the then inflects downward answering the question. "If you exercise regularly, then you'll improve your endurance."

Sometimes a word is missing, and the if-then structure is implied, like this line from Proteus in *The Two Gentlemen of Verona* where the "then" is implied before the word "teach":

> O sweet-suggesting Love, if thou hast sinned [THEN]
> Teach me (thy tempted subject) to excuse it.

Sometimes the if-then structure might be inverted, with the "then" coming before the "if." When you notice this, ask yourself: Is the character getting carried away emotionally or in some other way getting ahead of themselves? That's likely the case in this example from *The Taming of the Shrew*.

> KATE: Asses are made to bear, and so are you.
> PETRUCHIO: Women are made to bear, and so are you.
> KATE: No such jade as you, if me you mean.

If Kate's emotions were more balanced at this moment, she would more likely say something like: "If you mean me, then no such jade as you."

When you see an if-then statement—fully stated, implied, or inverted—it's helpful to ask yourself: Can the question-to-answer pitch pattern apply? If it can, it will communicate clearly to the audience's ears while adding some pitch variety to the performance, even when the if-then is inverted. Experiment with Kate's last line using this pitch pattern. THEN "No such jade as you, if me you mean."

NOUNS AND VERBS

Thoughts are often about one thing doing something to another thing. Making those connections evident to the listener is a big part of clarity. If the audience listens to your nouns and verbs, they will likely perceive the point of your thought. Choice and emphasis can help us.

Let's look at the nouns. Here's a short section from Berowne's earlier Act 3 speech. Go ahead and read this aloud.

> . . . it is a plague
> That Cupid will impose for my neglect,
> Of his almighty dreadful little might.

The nouns are: "plague," "Cupid," "neglect," and "might." When the actor emphasizes or in other ways uses these words, we're likely to hear the character's point of view on the subject and the line will communicate clearly. Read it aloud again, emphasizing the nouns which are in bold below. Generally, you want to avoid emphasizing pronouns.

> . . . it is a **plague**
> That **Cupid** will impose for my **neglect**,
> Of his almighty dreadful little **might**.

It gives the actor something to play and keeps this part of the thought clear.

Verbs are also helpful, especially action verbs. Let's take a look at Portia's speech. The action verbs are underlined. Go ahead and read this aloud emphasizing the underlined words. It's one thought, so try to keep your inflection up until reaching the full stop.

> In terms of choice I am not solely <u>led</u>
> By nice direction of a maiden's eyes:
> Besides, the lottery of my destiny
> <u>Bars</u> me the right of voluntary choosing:
> But if my Father had not <u>scanted</u> me,
> And <u>hedged</u> me by his wit to <u>yield</u> myself
> His wife, who <u>wins</u> me by that means I <u>told</u> you,
> Yourself (renowned prince) then <u>stood</u> as fair
> As any comer I have <u>looked</u> on yet
> For my affection.

Again, we have something to play.

Though this book doesn't address scansion in detail, we can use it to test and validate our noun and verb choices. Below, Portia's speech has been broken into two syllable feet. You'll also notice some feminine endings. The stressed syllables are in bold, and the verbs remain underlined. Note how many of the action verbs are both in bold and underlined.

> In **terms**/ of **choice**/ I **am**/ not **sole**/ly <u>**led**</u>/
> By **nice**/ dir**ect**/ion **of**/ a **mai**/den's **eyes**:/
> **Be**sides, / the **lot**/ery of/ my **des**/tin y
> <u>**Bars**</u> me/ the **right**/ of **vol**/un**tar**/y **choos**/ing:
> But **if**/ my **Fath**/er **had**/ not <u>**scant**</u>/ed **me**, /

And **hedged**/ me **by**/ his **wit**/ to **yield**/ my**self**/
His **wife**, / who **wins**/ me **by**/ that **means**/ I **told**/ you,
Your **self**/ (re**nown**/ed **Prince**)/ then **stood**/ as **fair**/
As **an**/y **com**/er **I**/ have **looked**/ on **yet**/
For **my**/ af**fect**/ion.

The verbs fall on the stressed syllables. It's like Shakespeare is using the iambic pentameter to encourage us to use the action verbs. Let's put the nouns in italics and see which of those fall on stressed syllables. The verbs remain underlined.

In *terms*/ of *choice*/ I **am**/ not **sole**/ly **led**/
By **nice**/ di*rect*/ion **of**/ a *mai/den's* *eyes*:/
Besides, / the *lot*/ery of/ my *des/tin* **y**
Bars me/ the **right**/ of **vol**/un**tar**/y *choos*/ing:
But **if**/ my *Fath*/er **had**/ not **scant**/ed me, /
And **hedged**/ me **by**/ his *wit*/ to **yield**/ my**self**/
His *wife*, / who **wins**/ me **by**/ that **means**/ I **told**/ you,
Your **self**/ (re**nown**/ed *Prince*)/ then **stood**/ as **fair**/
As **an**/y *com*/er **I**/ have **looked**/ on **yet**/
For **my**/ af*fect*/ion.

Most of the nouns also fall on stressed syllables, and, like stressed syllables, not all nouns are equally important. In the first line of Portia's speech, the noun "choice" is probably more important than the noun "terms" since the subject of this speech is how Portia is permitted to choose. However, the subject of "terms" is important throughout *The Merchant of Venice* since a lot of the plot hinges on the terms of business contracts.

If the actor speaking can emphasize, choose, or in other ways use select nouns and verbs to connect the thoughts, then the other words can support the main point of the line. Once we establish that primary narrative, we can more fully put our attention into other areas that'll enhance the entertainment value.

MODIFIERS

When speaking descriptive passages, we are speaking to the listeners' eyes—we want them to hear the words and see in their mind's eye what the character is seeing. Modifying words such as adjectives and adverbs should support—not eclipse—the noun or verb. This will help the audience visualize specific images while not confusing meaning. Here's Berowne's section again, this time with the descriptors underlined:

> . . . it is a plague
> That Cupid will impose for my neglect,
> Of his almighty dreadful little might.

The words "almighty," "dreadful," and "little" support the word "might." They help the listener visualize the kind of might Cupid possesses. They help us see a particular kind of Cupid. Were the actor to put their emphasis on "dreadful" at the expense of "might," for example, it would likely confuse the audience because we'd hear "dreadful" but not fully understand what he's talking about. Beware of any choice that clouds a speech's clarity.

"Might" is also the last word in the verse line and of the thought. In Shakespeare, these last words are often very important for the listener's comprehension.

KEY TAKEAWAYS: CLARITY

- Full stops help us discern the number and complexity of thoughts in a scene or speech.

- Simple thoughts and complex thoughts should be spoken differently.
- The number and length of thoughts in a speech has a profound impact on a character's rhythm.
- Upward inflection helps the listener know when the character has more to say. Downward inflection lets the listener know that the thought is about to finish.
- The stressed syllables within a line of blank verse do not require the same level of emphasis. Don't sound like a robot.
- Prose can provide latitude for the character to pause, improvise, or in other ways adapt to what is happening to the audience in real-time.
- If-then structure has a useful pitch pattern associated with it.
- Nouns and verbs tell the story. Emphasizing, choosing, and using these words keeps the meaning of the line clear.
- Modifying words will usually support the noun or verb rather than overwhelm it.
- The last words in the verse line or thought is often important for clarity.

VARIETY

You can already see how investing in clarity begins to create variety. Useful pitch patterns, use of nouns and verbs, and differentiating our simple and complex thoughts start us on that journey. When you're speaking complex thoughts, however, there is additional variety within the heightened language, and, like every part of Shakespeare's comedic design, it can provide opportunities we can take advantage of.

USEFUL SOUNDS

Not all sounds are equal when it comes to humor. Below is a quick list of some sounds to be on the lookout for in both prose and verse. If they're repeated, it's useful to explore them in rehearsal with emphasis and choice.

- The K sound, kuh. This is a funny sound and the strongest sound in English. This sound can be made with k, c, ch, and q. "Queen" and "Christmas" both have "k" sounds for example, as do "king," "country," and "cuckold."
- The F sound, fuh. F is the first letter in a number of our favorite words, including "fuck" and "falafel." Like kuh, it can also be funny. Why is the word "fish" funnier than "salmon"? The fuh sound has something to do with that.
- The P and B sounds, puh and buh. These plosive sounds are funny in part because of what they cause a person's mouth to do when speaking. If you see a string of Ps and Bs in Shakespeare's writing, ask yourself: Is this intended to be funny?
- The T sound, tuh. Ts can be used for insistence. If you see a string of Ts, ask yourself, am I driving the point home? In his book *Will Power*, John Basil notes that if a character is really getting carried away with T repetitions in a comedy, we should ask ourselves: Is the character spit-spraying?

You want as much variety in the performance as you can justify. When predominant sounds change within a speech or within a complicated thought, try changing your action. The change of action will sound justified if the actor is using the sounds and allowing them to impact their overall demeanor.

VOWELS CAN BE USEFUL TOO

I've heard that "vowels carry emotion, consonants carry information" from numerous teachers, and there's something to that assertion. When experimenting with vowel sounds in heightened language, take particular note of repeated long vowel sounds such as in "hay," "he," "hi," and "ho" and also short vowel sounds in words like "hat," "heck," "hit," and "hot." The geography of vowel progression within a speech can help us find the emotional journey. That can help inform the comedy as well.

Below is a fun thought to experiment with from Adriana's Act 2 speech in *The Comedy of Errors*. If you speak it with just the vowel sounds, omitting the consonants, you'll notice an interesting combination of shorter and longer vowel sounds.

> Aye, aye, Antipholus, look strange and frown,
> Some other mistress hath thy sweet aspects:
> I am not Adriana, nor thy wife.

This short exploration might pose good questions, like how long a vowel sound does "strange" want? But what you likely noticed is that the thought ends with three open vowel sounds on three monosyllabic words. Try building the thought and leaning into those three open sounds.

THE LOGIC IN A LIST

It's often the case that a list will build in emphasis. This applies to descriptors as well as nouns. This stepped-up, graduated build occurs regularly in heightened language—but not always. Rather than defaulting to a stepped-up build, a more useful question to ask yourself is: What is the logic in this list? For a short example, let's look at this line from Berowne's speech:

> Of his almighty dreadful little might.

It's a three-word list beginning with "almighty" and going to "dreadful" and "little," before arriving at the noun "might."

What is the logic in this list? Let's seek out playable variety because these three words mean very different things. If we were to speak them as if their meanings were the same, then we're losing an opportunity for variety. Over time, this can make the performance more predictable and less engaging.

While looking for the logic in this list you might notice a few things. You may notice the repetition of the word "might" in "almighty." Or you may notice the numerous T sounds in the line, with the D sounds in "dreadful" as an outlier. You might also notice the onomatopoetic nature of the words. "Almighty" "dreadful" and "little" can all sound like what they mean.

If the actor commits to the onomatopoeia in the list, the list gains variety. If the actor makes the word "almighty" sound like it is "All MIGHTY," and then speaks the word "dreadful" as if it were "DRRRrrread-ful" and then speaks "little" as if it were "little," we're on our way to crafting a detailed, more varied image: "Of his All MIGHTY dRRRrrread-ffful little might." This is a way to embody what John Basil would sometimes call the "geography of the line."

You might also notice that this line has a lot of T sounds in it. "Of his almighty dreadful little might." If the practitioners want to explore this observation, they'll notice that "dreadful" is lacking a T (though D is the voiced cousin of T). Is the logic of the list a same-to-DIFFERENT-to-same structure? Try leaning into that difference. "Of his almighty DREADffful little might." Or perhaps the literal difference in the meaning of the words is the way to go, and the structure is SAME-to-SAME-to-different structure?

Like we've already noted, the word "might" is repeated. Does the line simply want to be spoken with extra emphasis on the second "might"? "Of his al**mighty** dreadful little **might**."

When we scan the line we see that any of those choices can be backed up with the iambic pentameter. "Of **his**/ al**might**/y **dread**/ful **litt**/le **might**." There's more than one viable choice, and it's the practitioner's justification that will ultimately make the choice clear, believable, and compelling.

PUNCTUATION, AN INVITATION TO VARIETY

Effective comedy has a pleasing rhythm to it. A way into this rhythm is often through the punctuation. There's passion in punctuation. This applies to Shakespeare as well. Now, you might be thinking, "Hold on a second, didn't you just say that we can't know for sure what punctuation Shakespeare actually intended?" And you are correct: we cannot know for sure. But, despite this fact, using the punctuation provided in whatever version you're using is a useful tool on your interpretive journey. As you progress through your pre-production and rehearsal process, you can make necessary adjustments to support the aims of your production or simply to ensure clarity, reveal character, or increase entertainment value. It's not particularly useful to get hung up on what is "correct." So, let's assume that whoever put the punctuation into a certain line of your particular edition (the Elizabethan printer, modern editor, Shakespeare, etc.) that they knew something about theatre, story, and communication. We can always adjust punctuation if necessary.

Within complex lines of both prose and verse, you're likely to find commas, semicolons, and colons. Consider the punctuation you encounter helpful attempts by Shakespeare (or the editor) to guide you toward realizing the dramatic event. When working on complicated lines, it's important to remember to keep your inflection up so that the thought continues moving toward the full stop. Here's a brief explanation on using common punctuation within complex thoughts.

Commas are often like the word "and," which moves one part of the thought into the next part of the thought. Contemporary writers often use commas to denote parenthetical statements, but this is not always the case with Shakespeare. I encourage you to try using the comma as a springboard before defaulting to using it as a parenthetical. Your choice may become more nuanced and creative as a result.

A semicolon is like an emphatic "and." It's bigger than a comma and moves one part of the thought into the next part with more energy.

Colons often mark an attempt to clarify or explain what has been stated before the colon. It can be helpful to think of it as like the words "because" or "for example." A colon can easily sound like a full stop if the inflection goes downward, so the desire to move the thought forward until reaching the full stop is especially important.

Also, colons can mark places where physical business might be justified. This could be a bow, a false exit, a gesture, a change of focus, or another change in physical behavior. When seeing a colon in first folio punctuation, it's wise to ask yourself: Is there a gesture or business here? Let's take a look at this section of prose from Launce in *Two Gentleman of Verona*. I've added some colon-inspired direction in *italics* within [brackets].

> I am but a fool, look you, and yet I have the wit to think my master is a kind of a knave: [*use this colon to clarify the previous phrase with this next one*] but that's all one, if he be but one knave: [*after joke lands, false exit up left, then turn downstage*] He lives not now that knows me to be in love, yet I am in love, but a team of horse shall not pluck that from me: [*another false exit up left, before turning downstage again*] nor who 'tis I love: [*delivered like a tag line before presenting a cameo, about to exit stage left, then a bold, different, cross back downstage center*] and yet

'tis a woman; but what woman, I will not tell myself: [*Just stands there a moment, then steps toward audience to clarify*] and yet 'tis a milkmaid: [*lets that land, then clarify*] yet 'tis not a maid: [*for example*] for she hath had gossips: [*clarify*] yet 'tis a maid, for she is her master's maid, and serves for wages. She hath more qualities than a water spaniel, which is much in a bare Christian: [*lets that land, then on impulse takes a small scrap of paper from pocket*] Here is the cate-log of her condition. Inprimis. She can fetch and carry: [*use indicative gesture*] why a horse can do no more; nay, a horse cannot fetch, but only carry, therefore is she better than a jade. Item. She can milk, look you, a sweet virtue in a maid with clean hands.

These are just some colon-inspired options; you can make other choices as your imagination and technique inspires you. Within the above piece, you may have noticed other opportunities to utilize the punctuation and the other key lessons we've discussed so far. We'll revisit Launce again in the next chapter.

EXERCISE: PUNCTUATION WALK

Time for the full exercise! Like the earlier full-stop version, this exercise is a simple and effective way to embody the line. Working on Berowne, Portia, or a speech of your choosing, continue to change direction and action when you come to a full stop. Then, in addition to doing that, when you come to a comma, keep your inflection up as you do a quick skip-hop off one foot. For a semicolon, make it a bigger jump forward using both legs. When you encounter a colon, make a 90-degree right angle turn; colons are often pivots in the thought. If you have a parenthetical phrase, crouch. Physicalizing the changes will help you commit to the variety the writer has given you. Physicalizing helps us embody the geography of the line.

KEY TAKEAWAYS: VARIETY

- Useful sounds and repeated sounds help us find changes of action and emotional condition within complex lines.
- Each list has a logic to it that can inspire choices.
- Commas and semi-colons propel one part of the thought into the next part similar to the word "and."
- Colons frequently mark a point of clarification within the thought. Colons can also mark places for gestures, crosses, and other kinds of physical business.

HUMOR

Our work in clarity and variety has positioned us well to capitalize on the humor in Shakespeare's comedic design.

JOKE STRUCTURE

The simplest explanation of a verbal joke that I've heard is from the gifted acting teacher, Lesly Kahn. She described this structure as "same, same, different." This helps to make clear why it's said that comedy comes in three. The first two "sames" create an expectation that is then disrupted by the "different." Here's an opportunity from Proteus in *The Two Gentlemen of Verona*:

> To leave my Julia; shall I be forsworn?
> To love fair Silvia; shall I be forsworn?
> To wrong my friend, I shall be much forsworn.

If we speak the third "forsworn" differently than the previous two "forsworns," we have a joke. There's also a same, same, different with the verbs. "Leave" and "love" are both L words, and "wrong" sounds very different, perhaps even wrong relative to the other two. If we speak them all the same, it's harder for the joke to play.

Even when the humor doesn't come in threes, it's useful to ask yourself: Where are the "sames" and where is the "different"? How can you create expectations in your audience that you can then disrupt? Where are the opportunities for delightful surprise in Shakespeare's comedic design?

REPEATED SOUNDS, WORDS, AND PHRASES

Repetitions need to be recognized and utilized. Sometimes they set up the same, same, different structure like we just saw with "leave," "love," and "wrong." In Shakespeare, characters tend to repeat the words and sounds that are helping them get their needs met, that are helping them win. As John Basil would frequently say, "repeat the word the second time because it sounded so good the first time." You can use repetitions to justify a more varied and possibly humorous choice. You may want to build each repetition of a word in emphasis, or you can experiment with saying the repeated words differently from one another. A fun speech to play with is Edmund's famous "bastard" speech from Act 1 of *King Lear*.

> Thou Nature art my goddess, to thy law
> My services are bound, wherefore should I
> Stand in the plague of custom, and permit
> The curiosity of nations, to deprive me?
> For that I am some twelve, or fourteen moonshines
> Lag of a brother? Why bastard? Wherefore base?
> When my dimensions are as well compact,
> My mind as generous, and my shape as true
> As honest madam's issue? Why brand they us
> With base? With baseness bastardy? Base, base?
> Who in the lusty stealth of nature, take bastardy
> More composition, and fierce quality,
> Then doth within a dull stale tired bed
> Go to th' creating a whole tribe of fops
> Got 'tween a sleep, and wake? Well then,
> Legitimate Edgar, I must have your land,
> Our father's love, is to the bastard Edmond,

> As to th' legitimate: fine word: legitimate.
> Well, my legitimate, if this letter speed,
> And my invention thrive, Edmond the base
> Shall to' th' legitimate: I grow, I prosper:
> Now gods, stand up for bastards."

Edmund speaks a version of the word "bastard" five times within twenty-two lines. You should experiment with saying each of them differently. These same twenty-two lines also contain over a dozen other B words such as "base" and "brother." These sounds can also be used to help the character win. If you see three B words in close succession, is there an opportunity for the same, same, different structure explained earlier? With so many B sounds, does the character have a sense of humor? Is he sharing his humor with the audience? Edmund also speaks the word "legitimate" five times. There's a profound difference between the plosive B sounds of "bastard" and the little dance of T sounds in "legitimate." Do you discover anything if you lean into that difference?

UNUSUAL WORDS

Unusual words are a performance opportunity. "Fadge" is not an everyday word. Just because it's in a Shakespeare play doesn't mean that you have to speak "fadge" as if you say it daily. Employ your tools of choice and emphasis to use unusual words to fulfil the desired impact of Shakespeare's comedic design: to entertain today's audience. Unusual words will often want more relish or pleasure in the speaking of them than everyday words.

MALAPROPISM

Malapropism is when a character uses a similar sounding incorrect word in place of the grammatically correct word.

Shakespeare's malaprop characters were associated with the performance style of Will Kemp, and Shakespeare continued to employ malapropism even after Kemp's departure. When the character Dogberry scolds the villains Conrad and Borachio, he says, "O villain! thou wilt be condemned into everlasting redemption for this." He means "damnation" but says "redemption," and that's funny.

Malapropism is amusing for an audience as long as the audience is confident that the actor knows what the character is intending to say. It's important that prior to the malapropism that the actor has been comprehensible with their other dialogue. Using malapropism effectively requires conviction in what the character is trying to communicate.

SEXUAL HUMOR

Sexual appetite is vitality. It's the human spirit insisting on being reborn again and again. In spite of war, plague, famine, and tyranny, humanity is still kicking because we keep having sex. It's our collective way of refusing to die. Sex can make us feel a lot of different things; that's part of what makes it so dramatically interesting. Sex can be loving, funny, vulgar, violent, erotic, and more. It can be transcendently pleasurable, elegant, ridiculous, or just plain yucky. Dramatically, it's important that references to sex aren't ignored or apologized for. In Shakespeare's world, adults were expected to have a sexual appetite. Married people were expected to have sex with one another. It was considered unnatural for them not to. Sex is part of what most characters are expected to do after marriage.

Shakespeare references sex in his plays for various impacts. It can be referenced for humor; it can be referenced to reveal character. Characters can talk about sex poetically, using the topic of sex to connect one's passion to Nature's regenerative cycles. At other times, characters can talk of sex in baser terms, describing anatomy, sexually transmitted infections, and copulation with vulgar words and images. They're all part of the human experience.

The glimmer that exudes from the actor when hinting, eluding, or implying things of a sexual nature can be useful for the production and entertaining for the audience. Daring to reference sex more blatantly can also be useful. Shocking another character, or making an audience gasp, can bring them viscerally into the world of play. They might even feel complicit in being naughty. An important question for actor and director: Why is Shakespeare referencing sex at this point in the story? Why in this way?

Shakespeare, like other Elizabethan writers, employs gendered words. Some of these words are dated now, but we need to be on the lookout for them because they can lead us toward compelling choices and a fuller realization of Shakespeare's intentions. Is it a joke? Is it a promise? Is human vitality roaring into the play? You want to recognize sex in the writing and utilize it in a way that illuminates the play and pleases your audience. Does the poetry hint at the obscene, or is sex more blatantly referenced? How can we identify and embody the intentions of the writer?

MALE WORDS

In general, anything that looks phallic. A non-exhaustive list of male words:

- bold
- bugle
- dagger
- fish
- fool

- horn (phallic)
- launce
- shank
- sun
- will

A man's penis is his will. When he "wills" something, it can be useful to think of it as more than just a mental act; he's backing up his actions with his penis.

FEMALE WORDS

In general, anything round, wet, breast-like, or that can spread. A non-exhaustive list of female words:

- bird
- eye
- flower
- low country
- moon
- mountains
- pond
- ring
- Venus
- virtue

A woman's virtue was associated with her virginity, faithfulness, and genitalia. When she vows by her "virtue," she is often declaring her fidelity or virginity.

OTHER IMPORTANT SEX WORDS

- Cuckold horns. The reference to cuckold horns isn't phallic. It relates to antlers and the mating privileges of

winning elk stags and similar herd animals. It's a form of mockery to put horns on the head of the man whose wife has been unfaithful.
- Death. Orgasm was known as the "little death," or *la petite mort* in French. When a character speaks of dying, are they hinting at orgasm?
- Green. It's useful to know that the color green was associated with prostitutes and prostitution.
- Bold. When a character talks of feeling bold, are they experiencing a literal or metaphorical swell in their genitals as well?

KEY TAKEAWAYS: HUMOR
- Seek ways to create a pattern and then delight your audience with a surprise.
- Unusual words, repeated words, and malapropism should be identified and used by the practitioners.
- Shakespeare uses sexuality in his writing in a wide range of ways. Practitioners should make a choice about the desired impact on the audience. There's an important difference between playing the sexuality as a poetic expression of human vitality versus something more blatant.

CAUTIONS

It's important to justify all choices so that the action remains plausible within the given circumstances. Malapropism runs the risk of confusing your audience. Be clear and confident with what the character is intending to say as well as what the character actually speaks.

Character Studies

Six

INTRODUCTION

Let's see how these lessons might play out with a selection of roles in Shakespeare's comedies. Quick reminder: this book doesn't propose a linear, all-encompassing creative process to replace your preferred acting or directing technique. Rather, this book offers independent lessons that aim to help you ask more productive questions earlier in your creative process. The key lessons you've learned in these pages may or may not apply to each role and production you're working on. There are many delightful variables in the making of successful theatre, and we're wise to embrace the unique performance opportunities presented by each production.

In this chapter, we'll discuss six characters from six of Shakespeare's plays. It'll be useful to have a copy of the plays in question handy in case you want to reference the character or scenes discussed. All punctuation in quoted material is from Shakespeare's first folio. The act and scene breaks noted are also from the first folio. All spelling and capitalizations have been modernized.

The roles and characters we'll look at are:

- Don Armado in *Love's Labour's Lost*
- Launce in *The Two Gentlemen of Verona*
- Bottom in *A Midsummer Night's Dream*

- Feste in *Twelfth Night*
- Pompey in *Measure for Measure*
- Cloten in *Cymbeline*

We'll look to employ the key lessons from the previous five chapters. In particular:

- to unlock creative opportunities based on our understanding of Elizabethan sensibilities and theatre conventions;
- to identify and exploit any Commedia dell'arte influences;
- to detect principal comedian possibilities within the character;
- to locate Kemp's or Armin's performance aesthetics in the role;
- to note where we can employ lessons and techniques from the clown world;
- to identify and capitalize on useful language opportunities.

DON ARMADO, *LOVE'S LABOUR'S LOST*

One of Shakespeare's earliest comedies, *Love's Labour's Lost* is the story of the King of Navarre and his three noblemen friends. They swear off pursuing women and other frivolity for a period of three years so they can devote themselves to their studies. Of course, the Princess of France and her three gentlewomen arrive shortly after these oaths are made, and hilarity ensues as the men break their oaths and behave progressively more ridiculously as they woo their French female counterparts.

The court of Navarre is also the home of a "fantastical" Spaniard, Don Armado. Armado provides comic relief throughout the production as he grapples with his own affection for the "base wench" Jacquenetta. Don Armado appears in four scenes.

ACT 1, SCENE 2

In this scene, we learn that Don Armado is Spanish, considers himself a good soldier, is insecure in his love for Jacquenetta, and is written to be funny. He too has taken an oath to study with the King of Navarre, and he seeks to excuse his transgression for falling in love by making note of the famous men throughout history who have loved (Hercules, Sampson, etc.). We also learn that Moth is servant to Don Armado and in general considers his master, Don Armado, to be comically foolish.

ACT 3, SCENE 1

Here, the master–servant relationship between Don Armado and Moth is further developed through clever banter. We also learn more of Armado's affection for Jacquenetta.

ACT V, SCENE 1

Here, Don Armado inspires the impromptu play *The Nine Worthies*, which is hatched by the local teacher, Holofernes. This is in response to the King of Navarre ordering Armado to arrange the evening's entertainment for the court.

ACT V, SCENE 2

This is the longest scene in the play and its finale. Armado portrays the character Hector in the play-within-a-play *The Nine Worthies*. The king's court makes fun of Armado, Holofernes, and other members of their impromptu amateur theatre company. Their performance collapses in total when Costard announces that Jacquenetta is pregnant and accuses

Armado of fathering the child. Armado challenges Costard to a duel, but soon after we learn of the King of France's death. At that time, Armado and the other worthies exit. Armado and the others rejoin the action at the end of the play to sing two songs.

IS THERE A COMMEDIA INFLUENCE WE CAN CAPITALIZE ON?

Yes, in two major ways. First, Don Armado is clearly derived from the Commedia stock character Capitano. Indeed, his speech prefix in the first folio is "Brag.," almost certainly short for "Braggart." Second, the master–servant relationship between Armado and Moth is also core to Commedia's sensibilities, with Moth distinctly cleverer than his employer.

Don Armado also mentions his sword and fencing moves several times throughout the play. This is an opportunity to build a relationship of bravado with that prop, as well as lazzi concerning rituals of threats and combat preparations straight from the Capitano playbook. Shakespeare's audience would have recognized this character and expected lazzi and other lines of comic business as a result. In Act V, scene 2, Armado's bravado gives way to Capitano-inspired cowardice when he refuses to duel with Costard, completing that archetypal character's well-traveled braggart-to-coward arc.

Armado's interactions with his servant Moth are also humorous. We see Moth outwit him in various word games throughout the play. We also see where Armado's threat of punishment restores the Commedia status hierarchy in this relationship as well.

> ARMADO: . . . *Thou heat'st my blood.*
> MOTH: *I am answered, sir.*
> ARMADO: *I love not to be crossed.*

Moth then has to find new ways to mock his master Don Armado behind his back.

There are opportunities throughout the play to develop short lazzi related to different Capitano-like activities such as preparing to address Jacquenetta, threatening to punish Moth, how he celebrates getting an idea, and how he references his sword as well.

Throughout the play, Don Armado uses very elaborate and overly formal language. This is in keeping with the Capitano being a foreigner and traditionally Spanish in the Commedia universe. With English as his second language, Armado periodically uses language that is inappropriate for the situation, such as when he says the king dallies "with my excrement" when referencing his mustache.

CAN WE USE ANY LORD OF MISRULE OR FOOL INFLUENCES?

Indirectly. Don Armado is a foreign foil for Costard and Moth within the play. Costard was played by Kemp, the Lord of Misrule incarnate, and Costard was written to cement his bond with the audience during his remuneration speech in Act 3, scene 1. Moth embodies more of Commedia's clever servant tradition. Outwitting and duping Don Armado helps Costard and to a degree Moth unleash the periodic chaos we associate with the Lord of Misrule. This is especially evident in Act V, scene 2 when *The Nine Worthies* is completely usurped by the news of Jacquenetta's pregnancy.

WAS DON ARMADO WRITTEN FOR KEMP OR ARMIN?

Neither. Kemp played Costard, and Armin was not yet a member of Shakespeare's acting company. Don Armado is the only character we discuss in this chapter that was definitely not played by the play's principal comedian. However, in *Love's Labour's Lost*, Armado is the first character to be alone with the audience. Establishing that bond early in Act 1, scene 2 helps the audience look forward to his return throughout the play.

CAN WE EMPLOY LESSONS FROM THE CLOWN WORLD?

Yes. Don Armado and Moth's entrance at the top of Act 1, scene 2 can set the tone for them throughout the entire play. Though they are not in direct contact with their audience until later in the scene, the top of the scene is an opportunity for their costumes, particularly Armado's foreign clothes and total image, to impact the audience. Don Armado begins the scene by saying he is melancholy. This provides justification for the actor playing Armado to craft a lazzi embodying the "comedy of melancholy" for his entrance. Using a cameo at the end of Act 1, scene 2 and during the other scenes throughout the play can help the actor strengthen the bond between character and audience as well.

We've already mentioned lazzi related to Capitano possibilities, but there are more opportunities. Armado is in love, and, though this lazzi is more associated with the young lover stock characters than a captain, how might Armado prepare himself to address his beloved Jacquenetta?

Don Armado's costume from his first entrance should appear foreign and fantastical and visually distinguish him from the other characters in the play. There is additional opportunity to capitalize on costume in Act V, scene 2 when Armado enters as Hector during *The Nine Worthies*.

WHAT ARE THE LANGUAGE OPPORTUNITIES?

Don Armado has some very humorous language, and he's written almost entirely in prose with the rhythmic freedom that form provides. We've already mentioned the overly formal word choice and occasional accidental inuendo.

Armado's speech in Act V, scene 1 is instructive. At this point, the audience has bonded with him and expects the character to speak and in other ways behave in certain ways. In this speech, Armado addresses Holofernes and eventually asks him for help.

> Sir, the king is a noble gentleman, and my familiar, I do assure ye very good friend: for what is in-ward between us, let it pass. I do beseech thee remember thy courtesy. I beseech thee apparel thy head: and among other importunate and most serious designs, and of great import indeed too: but let that pass, for I must tell thee it will please his grace (by the world) sometime to lean upon my poor shoulder, and with his royal finger thus dally with my excrement, with my mustachio: but sweetheart, let that pass. By the world I recount no fable, some certain special honors it pleaseth his greatness to impart to Armado a soldier, a man of travel, that hath seen the world: but let that pass; the very all of all is: but sweetheart I do implore secrecy, that the king would have me present the princess (sweet chuck) with some delightful ostentation, or show, or pageant, or antick, or fire-work: now, understanding that the curate and your sweet self are good at such eruptions, and sudden breaking out of mirth (as it were) I have acquainted you withal, to the end to crave your assistance.

In this speech, we see Armado's foreignness on full display as he uses overly formal language, and particularly when he uses inappropriate terms of endearment, referring to his colleagues as "sweetheart" and "sweet chuck." We also hear him brag about his friendship with the king, and something like the Capitano's battle résumé lazzi when he describes himself a "soldier," a "traveler" and such. He uses a surprising number of titles. Armado also speaks the signature phrases "let that pass" as well as the earlier mentioned "excrement."

LAUNCE, *THE TWO GENTLEMEN OF VERONA*

The Two Gentlemen of Verona is another early Shakespeare comedy, possibly Shakespeare's first. It tells the story of two pairs of young heterosexual lovers as they negotiate a love triangle between Valentine, Sylvia, and Proteus. Eventually Proteus returns his affections to his betrothed Julia, and Valentine is able to secure the blessing of Sylvia's father for his upcoming marriage to her. By the end of the play, the couples are reunited in sincere love with their "natural" matches and all ends happily.

Proteus's servant, Launce, provides comic relief throughout the play as he negotiates leaving his home in Verona for the big city of Milan. We also learn of his developing love life with a local milkmaid, and the antics of his dog, Crab.

Please note that some of Launce's dialogue is antisemitic. I strongly encourage practitioners to change these unfortunate words or consider omitting those lines altogether from the performance except under very deliberate, non-harmful conditions.

Launce appears in at least four scenes.

ACT 2, SCENE 3

Launce enters with his dog Crab and talks with the audience about saying farewell to his family and how indifferent the dog was during this tearful farewell. Launce is later beckoned to row in a boat in pursuit of his master Proteus's ship.

ACT 2, SCENE 5

Launce enters, again with his dog Crab, and is discovered by Valentine's servant, Speed. This is a short scene that furthers the plot while entertaining us with clever wordplay. Launce and Speed discuss Proteus and Julia's marriage engagement. Speed shares that his master Valentine is pursuing love in Milan.

ACT 3, SCENE 1

Launce enters with his master Proteus in search of Valentine. They discover Valentine, and Launce offers to fight him. Once the masters exit, Launce talks with the audience about the milkmaid he is in love with. This contrast of hearing Launce talk about the attributes of the milkmaid provides structural commentary after hearing Silvia praised by both Valentine and Proteus earlier. Speed enters and discovers Launce. They banter words laced with sexual innuendo.

ACT 4, SCENE 4

Launce enters, again with his dog Crab, to talk with the audience. We learn that Launce has taken the blame for Crab pissing on the floor of the banquet hall, and that Launce has been whipped "out of the chamber" as a result. We later learn that at the banquet Launce had presented his big dog Crab as a gift to Sylvia in place of the dainty "squirrel" of a dog his master Proteus had instructed him to give her. Proetus gets angry and sends Launce and Crab offstage.

This is the last scene where Launce appears unless the director stages a bergamask at the end of the play where Launce could reenter to celebrate the upcoming marriages. In this case, Launce might reenter with the milkmaid and show off Kemp's famous leaping ability prior to curtain call. The dog Crab could be involved too, perhaps appearing with the "squirrel" dog as his "natural" match. All ends happily.

IS THERE A COMMEDIA INFLUENCE WE CAN CAPITALIZE ON?

Yes. Launce is part of a master–servant relationship with Proteus. During the play, there is opportunity for Launce to respond to the threat of punishment from his master as he regularly bungles tasks, social interactions, and in other ways gets carried away. This is the case in Act 3, scene 1, when Launce offers to fight Valentine who has referred to himself as "nothing." Launce picks up this "nothing" and begins to ask Proteus if he (Launce) should strike Valentine (nothing) several times. This is a great opportunity to build justified lazzi. How might Launce prepare to fight? Does Launce practice jabs, chops, and body slams? How hard does Proteus have to work to control Launce's recently discovered passion to strike at "nothing"? The Lord of Misrule roars onto the stage!

When Launce presents the wrong dog to Silvia as a gift, it's a variation on the time-tested Commedia lazzi where an illiterate servant delivers the wrong letter to their master's beloved. Though this blundering of the gifted dog takes place offstage, Launce is scolded by his master Proteus onstage before being sent off to find the missing dog.

In addition to the master–servant dynamic described above, the relationship between Launce and his fellow servant Speed deserves mention. This easygoing relationship between fellow servants is in contrast to their more formal dialogues with their respective masters. It evokes classic comedic servant duos such as the relationship between the zanies Arlecchino and Brighella.

CAN WE USE ANY LORD OF MISRULE OR FOOL INFLUENCE?

Yes. Launce is written in the Lord of Misrule tradition. There are numerous opportunities throughout the play where Launce might appear to usurp the direction of the play and the overall narrative. This is clearly seen in sections where Launce becomes insistent on doing something or not doing something. For example in Act 2, scene 3, when Launce doesn't want to leave the stage and row after Proteus's ship. Another in Act 3, scene 1 when Launce is very intent on threatening Valentine with violence while Proteus is trying to have a conversation with him. Also, in Act 4, scene 4, when we hear that Launce took the blame for Crab urinating on the floor, the audience is invited to imagine the kind of anarchy Launce must have created during that formal occasion, even though it occurred offstage.

WAS LAUNCE WRITTEN FOR KEMP OR ARMIN?

Launce was written for Kemp. In many ways, Launce is textbook Kemp. He has the long monologue with the audience early in the play to facilitate bonding with the groundlings in a relationship of equals. That first monologue provides many opportunities to physicalize, and we experience Launce from the small town of Verona dealing with the complexities of the big city of Milan, part of the rustic clown tradition associated with Kemp. Launce has two other significant solo pieces that capitalize on this initial bond with the audience and allow Kemp to use his exceptional abilities in solo performance.

Also, knowing that Kemp was famous for his leaping ability, are there plausible opportunities to leap as part of the character's cameo presentation prior to exit? Even if the actor playing Launce is not an expert leaper, we can take inspiration from what we know of Kemp's celebrity. How can we boldly physicalize just prior to the exit?

CAN WE EMPLOY LESSONS FROM THE CLOWN WORLD?

Definitely. Launce's first solo monologue lends itself to Avner's technique for entering the stage and building a meaningful relationship with the audience. His first monologue in Act 2 also lends itself to something of a puppet show with the staff, dog, and shoes portraying the different family members as he acts out his farewell with his family. Presenting a cameo prior to exiting with the messenger in that scene should strengthen that bond. Mindfully crafted and performed, the relationship between Launce and the audience will be very strong by the end of that first scene.

Also, at the top of Act 4, scene 4, after Launce has been "whipped" out of the banquet, it would be justified for him to nurse his soreness after being struck and driven out of the room. How might he employ clown logic to tend to his injuries? The lazzi of a lump on the head? Further, in his first and last solo pieces with the audience, Launce is upset. In the first one, he talks at length about his tears. There are definite sad clown opportunities here. What is the comedy of despair?

The play also provides opportunities to develop relationship to costume and to present costume-based visual gags. For example, when Launce attends the banquet prior to Act 4, scene 4, how has he dressed up for the event? How has he prepared his dog Crab to be a gift as substitute for the stolen "squirrel dog"? For example, if Launce puts a bow on Crab's collar to make him appear more like a gift, then he may have added a bow tie to his own outfit so he might fit in better with the upper crust of Milanese society.

WHAT ARE THE LANGUAGE OPPORTUNITIES?

Launce is written in prose, giving Kemp room to play with rhythm and improvise as needed. His language regularly employs malapropism and both intentional and unintentional sexual inuendo. In Act 2, scene 3, the colons are great points of departure for Launce to gesture and physicalize the action. They're also useful for focus changes between the different characters in his puppet show. In this speech, many of the action verbs deserve attention as they can inform the physical action as well. There's a sex joke about the shoe with the hole in it representing his mother. The colons provide solid markers for stage business and focus shifts in Launce's Act 4, scene 4 speech as well.

In Act 2, scene 5, Launce's banter with Speed is peppered with erection jokes and a reference to sexually transmitted infection. We get to enjoy these two rascals gossiping and talking trash before heading to the alehouse.

In Act 3, scene 1, the opportunities for lazzi are largely marked by colons and question marks. It's wise for the production team to explore this part of the comedic design. There is malapropism speaking "vanished" in place of "banished." After Launce catalogs the virtues and faults of the milkmaid, Speed enters. The banter between the two is peppered with sexual inuendo around words such as "spin," "another thing," and "purse," which reads as a synonym for "pussy." Their banter contains some clear examples of verbalized clown logic. Many opportunities to choose, emphasize, and sparkle in this scene.

BOTTOM, *A MIDSUMMER NIGHT'S DREAM*

A Midsummer Night's Dream is one of Shakespeare's most popular plays. It's unusual in that it consists of multiple subplots, and the play itself does not readily appear to have a clear, single, traditional protagonist. Bottom is part of the subplot where a group of amateur actors prepare their production with the hopes of being selected to perform as part of Duke Theseus's wedding celebration.

Bottom appears in five scenes.

ACT 1, SCENE 2

We learn that Bottom, the weaver, and the rest of the Mechanicals are competing to entertain Duke Theseus during his wedding reception. It establishes Bottom as an enthusiastic, amateur actor and that he has a place of prominence within the acting troupe.

ACT 3, SCENE 1

At the beginning of their rehearsal, Bottom meddles with the creation of the play to a ridiculous extent by insisting that they add a Prologue to assure the women in the audience that what they're viewing is fiction. The magical fairy Puck turns Bottom into an ass. When Titania, the queen of the fairies, awakes from her slumber, she immediately falls in love with Bottom. This is due to the effects of a magic flower that was applied to Titania without her knowledge or consent. For the director, in addition to its humor, this scene provides structural commentary on the larger themes of love and courtship within the play. Previously we saw how the various young lovers pursue one another. Here we get to see Titania, queen of the fairies, pursue Bottom, the weaver.

ACT 4, SCENE 1

Bottom in a "flowery bed" with Titania, ordering her fairy servants about with tasks such as scratch his ears, get a honey bag from a bee, and let's hear country music with the "tongs and the bones." Bottom hungers for hay and other kinds of horse feed. The love spell on Titania is eventually lifted, and her love for Bottom vanishes. Titania exits with Oberon, the king of the fairies and Titania's "natural" match, leaving Bottom alone onstage. Bottom is turned back into himself and awakes as if from a dream. Alone, he speaks to the audience about his dream.

ACT 4, SCENE 2

Bottom is reunited with his fellow Mechanicals and possesses the knowledge necessary to accelerate the plot: that their play is "preferred" and that they must prepare for their performance at Duke Theseus's wedding reception. How Bottom hears this news is never fully explained in the script.

ACT 5, SCENE 1

Bottom and the rest of the amateur actors perform their play to the best of their abilities while the nobles playfully ridicule their efforts. Structurally, for the director, we see two commentaries. One is on the making of a play and what can happen when amateurs attempt work best done by professionals. The other is on the theme of courtship and wooing. After seeing the young lovers of Athens woo in various combinations, and witnessing Titania the Fairy Queen woo Bottom, here in this play-within-a-play we see the "tragic" wooing of Pyramus and Thisbe. But because the tragic nature of this wooing is portrayed by Bottom and Flute, the wooing and lamenting quickly become ridiculous.

IS THERE A COMMEDIA INFLUENCE WE CAN CAPITALIZE ON?

Some, but not a lot. Though Bottom would be part of the servant class in the Commedia universe, he doesn't really serve a master during the action. He has an inflated sense of his abilities as an actor, which in some ways can resemble a Capitano bragging, but the chief difference between them is that the Capitano knows that he's lying whereas Bottom seems to truly believe that he's an exceptionally talented actor. Bottom does respect the nobility during the last scene when performing in the play-within-a-play. He also happily accepts the master status afforded him in Queen Titania's court while in her favor. At her court, and as an ass, he exhibits significant hunger, in some ways similar to the servants of the Commedia. The difference is that Bottom is literally hungry as a horse. Or, rather, as hungry as an ass.

CAN WE USE ANY LORD OF MISRULE OR FOOL INFLUENCE?

Certainly. Bottom is written in the Lord of Misrule tradition. Throughout the play, Bottom cultivates and unleashes chaos by usurping the conventional status hierarchy. When Queen Titania, under the influence of the magic flower, falls in love with Bottom, she refers to him as a "gentlemen" and gives him authority to command her servants. Like a Lord of Misrule given the run of the court for a week, Bottom turns the fairy court on its head and becomes a very demanding, albeit temporary, aristocrat.

But Bottom shows his Lord of Misrule inclinations from the start of the play when usurping Peter Quince's authority during the Mechanicals' rehearsal with his numerous interjections such as "let me play Thisbe too." Bottom continues his usurping behaviors during their next scene prior to his transmutation into an ass. These attempts at usurping continue while playing Pyramus in the play's final scene. Here he breaks the fourth wall and addresses Duke Theseus and his court directly to comment on the action.

WAS BOTTOM WRITTEN FOR KEMP OR ARMIN?

Kemp. Kemp's longer monologue early in the play where he bonds with the audience is disguised in *Midsummer's* Act 1, scene 2, as a dialogue between Bottom and the rest of the actors. But Bottom does the majority of the talking. With an Elizabethan audience seated on three sides of the actors in universal lighting, it's easy to envision staging this scene so that the audience in the theatre "becomes" the other Mechanicals at the rehearsal. This would justify Bottom directly addressing the audience during the scene and forging that initial bond with them that we see so frequently in Kemp's roles.

As the play's action unfolds and more and more fantastical events happen to him, Bottom becomes the groundling's avatar, their representative onstage. He takes a journey that most of us can only dream of traveling.

CAN WE EMPLOY LESSONS FROM THE CLOWN WORLD?

Certainly. As mentioned in the previous section, the actor playing Bottom has opportunity to bond with the audience early. The modern director looking to capitalize on Shakespeare's comedic design can facilitate that bonding with appropriate staging. The production benefits if this process is complete prior to Bottom's huge status change, when he becomes lover to the queen of the fairies. Moments can be found in the text where the actor playing Bottom can share his onstage experiences with the audience and make them feel complicit in his actions.

There are opportunities for physical business with Bottom as well; often, but not always, on the colons in the first folio text. Short gags are possible when Bottom quickly demonstrates how he will play the different roles within the play such as Thisbe and Lion. The performance of their play is clearly intended to be ridiculous. Much of it doesn't require anything extra from the actors; simply wear the costume and speak the words with as much conviction as possible. Bottom and Flute are acting their hearts out, but the choice of words Shakespeare provides are silly. Some of the business with the character Wall is unintentionally bawdy related to striking and kissing Wall's "stones." Their play ends with Bottom portraying the suicide of Pyramus. The word "thus" is repeated several times in a row and can benefit from physical justification. Is there a gag that will please the audience that supports those repetitions? Maybe the dagger doesn't actually penetrate until the last "thus"?

The arc of Bottom's total visual image is also interesting:

- We see Bottom as a weaver.
- Bottom is turned into an ass.
- Adornments might be added to his outfit when he is brought into Queen Titania's fairy bower, reflecting his change in status.
- He is turned back into a working-class human.
- Bottom gets into costume so he can play Pyramus in the play-within-the-play.

This is quite the arc of images!

There's opportunity to design an initial costume that gives the audience permission to laugh but leaves room for the ass mask to escalate. The image can continue building its momentum with high-status adornments and then the costume for Bottom's Pyramus to be plausibly funnier than Bottom's regular weaver wear. The actor can allow the total image choices to play by finding moments of relative stillness as explained in Chapter 4.

Here are a few other opportunities. Kemp was not known for his singing ability. When Bottom's fellow Mechanicals desert him in the woods in Act 3, Bottom sings to show them that he is not afraid. Titania describes her reaction to Bottom's singing as being "enamored with your note." This can justify some terrible singing lazzi as long as it remains plausible. Titania is also impressed with Bottom's looks and his total being—basically everything he does—because of the magic flower's influence. Also, is Bottom about to speak when

Titania says "tie up my lover's tongue"? There's opportunity for lazzi here when Bottom, for the first time in the play, has nothing to say.

WHAT ARE THE LANGUAGE OPPORTUNITIES?

Bottom is written in prose. As already mentioned, there are useful colons in the folio text for the practitioners to create short physical lazzi, change focus, or simply share the events onstage with their audience.

Bottom employs a good amount of if-then logic. You'll recall from Chapter 5 that there is a pitch pattern associated with this structure and that it can provide the actor with a simple road map that contributes to the production's clarity and vocal variety.

Bottom also uses a lot of malapropism and has a lot of language jokes based in that. He also has a number of jokes related to transposed and repeated words, particularly at the end of the play where one gets the impression that he memorized his script incorrectly. On the whole, his language becomes more absurd as the play progresses. His nagging hunger for horse feed in Act 4, scene 1, asks for emphasis and choice, and possibly short signature gestures. Does he paw the ground with his hoof?

Some of Bottom's malaprops are unintentionally sexual in nature. Saying that the lion "deflowered" his Thisbe rather than "devoured" her is one. Rehearsing "obscenely" and references to a "French crown" meaning both a gold coin and venereal disease are others.

FESTE, TWELFTH NIGHT

Twelfth Night is one of Shakespeare's finest comedies. The language is beautiful and the characters delightful. The story is remarkably resilient in its simplicity and periodic juxtaposition of life-affirming love and desire with inevitable disappointments and death. The beauty of the play is experienced fuller as a result.

Feste appears in seven scenes.

ACT 1, SCENE 5

Feste begins with some verbal banter with Maria showcasing his wit and revealing important exposition. Momentarily alone, he speaks a short speech to Wit. Feste then continues his bantering with the mistress of the palace the Countess Olivia, then with Sir Toby, and finally with Malvolio who seems to get the better of him. This scene establishes several important relationships in Olivia's palace.

ACT 2, SCENE 3

After bantering with the intoxicated Sir Toby and Sir Andrew, Feste sings a song. Despite it being the middle of the night, the singing escalates into a group drinking song. These impromptu festivities bring Maria onstage, and are eventually ended by Malvolio. Upon Malvolio's exit, Feste, Toby, Andrew, and Maria agree to work together to dupe Malvolio.

ACT 2, SCENE 4

In this short scene, Feste sings for Duke Orsino in his palace. Orsino is in the company of the female Viola who is disguised as Orsino's serving man, Cesario. Feste demonstrates how cleverly he can ask for additional tips.

ACT 3, SCENE 1

This scene begins with an implied musical routine. When Viola (Cesario) enters, her first line is, "dost thou live by thy tabor?" Banter between the two continues with Viola ultimately tipping Feste. At that point, Feste employs his wit to beg more money from her.

ACT 4, SCENE 2

In this scene, Feste and the others humiliate Malvolio. Feste disguises himself as Sir Topas the curate and dialogues with himself in different voices out of the imprisoned Malvolio's sight in order to confuse and torment him. Feste ultimately exits in song, comparing himself to the vice characters found in medieval drama.

ACT 5, SCENE 1

This is the scene where all is revealed, and most is resolved. The scene begins with Feste tricking Fabian about the letter. Feste then fools with Orsino, earning more tips. He's then compelled to read the letter which he does with "vox" or a "madman's" voice. He ultimately reveals his Sir Topas imitation to Malvolio and later sings a song to end the play.

IS THERE A COMMEDIA INFLUENCE WE CAN CAPITALIZE ON?

Some. There is a master–servant dynamic at times between Feste and the play's aristocrats. Begging for tips, or in other ways using one's wit to make sure one is appropriately paid, is common in Commedia. Lazzi related to singing and letter reading is also justifiable.

CAN WE USE ANY LORD OF MISRULE OR FOOL INFLUENCE?

Definitely. Feste is a professional fool and regularly uses his fool's prerogative to step out of the play's status hierarchy. This is seen in how he plays with the Countess Olivia and, to a lesser extent, Duke Orsino. It is perhaps seen clearest in Act 1, scene 5 when Feste "proves" Olivia a fool for over-mourning her deceased brother.

Feste also references his costume as "patched," and this gives us a strong indicator that he is visually distinguished as both the principal comedian in the production and a professional fool by trade.

WAS FESTE WRITTEN FOR KEMP OR ARMIN?

Armin. Feste is textbook Armin, and we can see Shakespeare capitalize on Armin's performance strengths, particularly his well-regarded singing and mimicry, by weaving those skills into his comedic design. Feste sings several songs during the play, including the song that ends the play. Toby mentions that Feste "counterfeits" well.

Feste makes mention of his shorter size, and he rarely holds stage alone for a significant amount of time. We frequently see Feste working within a duologue or as part of a small group or trio.

CAN WE EMPLOY LESSONS FROM THE CLOWN WORLD?

Definitely. Early in the play, we experience Feste's high-status relationship to the other characters onstage as he regularly outwits them for the pleasure of the audience (and his own). Within that early action in Act 1, scene 5, Feste briefly holds stage alone, beseeching Wit to aid him in his upcoming encounter with the Countess Olivia. This is a short but important opportunity for the actor playing Feste to establish contact with the audience in a position of vulnerability. This important first step with the audience is then strengthened when we see Feste return to his professional fool persona upon Olivia's entrance. The audience then has an opportunity to know that there's a real, vulnerable human being under all that wit.

Feste wears at least two costumes in the play. The first, his professional fool uniform, is a version of the "patched" motley. At Maria's request, Feste changes his image when he puts on a gown and beard to take on the role of Sir Topas during the duping and humiliation of Malvolio. There's entertainment potential for the actor when they develop a relationship with their costume. This potential tends to be greater in comedy, and maybe greatest in Shakespeare when the role was performed by the principal comedian.

Feste also has several opportunities for vocal bits, gags, and routines throughout the play including the songs mentioned earlier. These are supported by the text and can please the audience as they showcase the expertise of the performer.

The actor playing Feste should strongly consider developing a signature gesture so that when he triumphs in a battle of wits, he can then express his victory and satisfaction with that gesture. This will help the audience root for him and look forward to his next victory.

WHAT ARE THE LANGUAGE OPPORTUNITIES?

Feste is written in prose, but his language is quite complicated due to his wit and intelligence. He describes himself as a "corrupter of words," and this an excellent direction for modern practitioners to take to heart.

Feste's language employs a lot of if-then reasoning and also lists. Using pitch patterns, choice, and emphasis to maximize the entertainment in these sections is covered in Chapter 5. Feste also uses Latin, other foreign phrases, as well as implausibly complicated and increasingly ridiculous names.

When he does solicit for tips, Feste does so in a clever way. There is entertainment value in his solicitations. He never comes straight out and pleads for money. He's not a beggar;

he regularly demonstrates his expertise and expects to be paid for it.

POMPEY, *MEASURE FOR MEASURE*

Measure for Measure was written in the middle of Shakespeare's career and is often referred to as a problem play. It's classified as a comedy in the first folio, but its plot and themes are more serious and somber, and dramatized with more cruelty than one typically sees in Shakespeare's other comedies.

Measure for Measure presents the need to balance justice with mercy and appetite with restraint. The play's action is ultimately resolved, with the promise of both enthusiastic and reluctant marriages to follow. How the Duke's own marriage proposal to Isabelle is answered is open to interpretation because she doesn't answer him and then doesn't speak for the remainder of the play.

As you may remember from Chapter 4, Pompey is a pimp. He's eventually arrested by the authorities and spends the latter part of the play in jail. He appears in five scenes.

ACT 1, SCENE 2

We meet Pompey, referenced as "Clo" in the first folio. He talks with a prostitute and shares that the brothels in Vienna's suburbs are to be closed and torn down by legal decree. Still, he's confident that prostitutes and pimps like themselves will continue to find work.

ACT 2, SCENE 1

Pompey has been arrested by the malaprop constable Elbow and is brought before the local authorities. After a good deal of verbal banter between Pompey, Elbow, and Escalus, we learn that Pompey has a large "bum." Escalus lets Pompey off with only a warning and advises him to mend his criminal ways.

ACT 3, SCENE 2
Pompey has been arrested again. About to answer to the magistrate, he sees Lucio, a gentlemen and frequenter of Pompey's former establishment. Pompey ask Lucio to bail him out of jail. Lucio teases Pompey, and ultimately refuses to bail him out.

ACT 4, SCENE 2
We discover Pompey in the prison. The provost convinces Pompey to become the executioner's assistant rather than suffer a merciless whipping.

ACT 4, SCENE 3
Pompey begins onstage alone. He talks about how many of his former customers are also imprisoned, making jokes about their habits and sexually transmitted diseases. He talks with the executioner, Abhorson, whom he has assisted by setting the executioner's axe upon the chopping block. Pompey also dialogues with the prisoner Barnadine, who, along with Isabelle's brother, Claudio, is scheduled for execution that morning.

IS THERE A COMMEDIA INFLUENCE WE CAN CAPITALIZE ON?
Pompey is a common pimp, a servant willing to break the law to get ahead. This would make him a first Zanni in the Commedia universe. Also, the script references his "bum" and states that it's unusually large. Though an uncommonly large bum is not a mask per se, the cameo and other performance techniques associated with acting in mask can work for Pompey's total image.

CAN WE USE ANY LORD OF MISRULE OR FOOL INFLUENCE?

Yes. Though Pompey's a pimp by trade and not a professional fool, he is written with similar sensibilities. He's often the smartest character onstage, easily outwitting the malaprop constable Elbow. He speaks truth to power with Escalus. Pompey tells him that if he continues enforcing Vienna's sex laws so harshly that he will depopulate the city to such an extent that rents would fall and that even Pompey would be able to rent a palatial house. That would be significant disruption to Vienna's status hierarchy! Pompey also turns phrases in ways that point out human absurdities. When he becomes assistant to the prison's executioner, he facilitates the chaos that unfolds in the jail.

WAS POMPEY WRITTEN FOR KEMP OR ARMIN?

Pompey was very likely written with Armin in mind. In many ways he reads like a professional fool, just without the uniform. Pompey's unusual proportions ("your bum is the greatest thing about you") make us think of Armin's unusual look. Pompey doesn't speak his solo monologue with the audience until Act 4, and he shares the stage with the misspoken Elbow, the hedonist Lucio, and the authoritative Escalus, among others, in the first half of the play. This kind of small-group configuration is typical for roles likely written for Armin.

CAN WE EMPLOY LESSONS FROM THE CLOWN WORLD?

Yes. In Chapter 4, we discussed in some detail a possible routine for the executioner's axe and chopping block in Act 4, scene 3. There are other opportunities as well, particularly when letting his bum-centered image have a humorous impact on the audience.

WHAT ARE THE LANGUAGE OPPORTUNITIES?

Pompey is written in prose, and he banters throughout the play with other characters. He regularly proves his case while showcasing his skill with witty argumentation, proving the other characters—particularly law enforcement—"natural fools." It's important to note, however, those moments when he's not bantering. Pompey ceases his clever banter when events are going poorly for him, and these are places where the performance can take on more sincerity and vulnerability. Again, we can see that there's a real person underneath the wit.

Many of Pompey's lines contain sexual innuendo and *double entendres* such as "respected" and "groping for trout in a peculiar river" implying sexual intercourse, among other words and phrases. Pompey helps to make *Measure for Measure* one of Shakespeare's most sexual plays.

CLOTEN, *CYMBELINE*

Cymbeline is one of Shakespeare's later plays and is often referred to as a romance. This is a time in Shakespeare's career when he had already established himself as a master craftsperson of plays, and he was now experimenting more with form and content.

Cymbeline tells the story of Britain's emancipation from the Roman Empire. Within this larger political conflict is the love between Imogen, King Cymbeline's daughter, and Posthumus, an orphan and her newlywed husband. Several characters try to thwart that relationship. One of them is Cloten, Imogen's stepbrother, who wants to marry Imogen himself to cement his hereditary claim to England's throne. Cloten is hot-headed and enormously proud of himself.

Cloten appears in seven scenes.

ACT 1, SCENE 3

We learn that Cloten has a high opinion of himself and that others praise him to his face while ridiculing him behind his back. Cloten swears regularly, and we learn that he has an unusual odor. He rarely conducts himself in a dignified way, even though he's the queen's son.

ACT 2, SCENE 1

Cloten's relationship with Lord 1 and Lord 2 continues to show how these courtiers are two-faced in their dealings with him. Lord 2 references Cloten's odor again, saying that he smells "like a fool." Unsurprisingly, we hear more swearing from Cloten and learn that he frequently instigates violent conflicts.

ACT 2, SCENE 3

Cloten interacts with several characters in this scene. Again, we hear more references about him being a sore loser. He employs musicians to help him woo Imogen. He even sings a song for her. Momentarily alone with the audience, he explains his plan to bribe Imogen's servants. He subsequently banters with one of Imogen's waiting gentlewomen, most likely Helen. Imogen enters and insults him, saying she prefers Posthumus's humble garments to Cloten. Cloten becomes somewhat obsessed with this, and mentions those garments four times in response to her during the rest of the scene.

ACT 3, SCENE 1

Cloten joins with the king and with his mother, the queen, in defying Rome. He interrupts his mother and uses some taunting language toward the Roman diplomat.

ACT 3, SCENE 5

Cloten discovers that Imogen has fled the palace. He talks with the audience about how much he admires Imogen's beauty but hates her for not returning his admiration. Pisanio, Imogen's servant, enters, and Cloten threatens him with death unless he agrees to betray Imogen and serve him. Cloten sees a letter detailing Imogen's plans and then asks Pisanio for Posthumus's clothes. Alone onstage, Cloten then shares his fantasy for revenge with the audience. In this fantasy, he will kill Posthumus, sexually assault Imogen, and do all of this while wearing Posthumus's clothes.

ACT 4, SCENE 1

Cloten compares himself to Posthumus and explains his plan to behead Posthumus, "enforce" Imogen, and tear up Posthumus's clothes before "spurning" Imogen home to the castle.

ACT 4, SCENE 2

Hoping to come across Imogen in the wilderness outside the castle, Cloten instead encounters Guiderius. Cloten insults him numerous times before attacking him with "die the death." The combat takes them offstage where Guiderius kills Cloten. Cloten's head is brought back onstage. Imogen is brought onstage unconscious by Guiderius's kinsman, Arviragus. They think her dead and lay her out for legitimate burial rights. They then bring Cloten's headless body onstage and lay it next to her for similar burial rights. They exit, leaving Imogen, who they still think is dead, alone with Cloten's headless corpse. She awakes, and, because he's wearing Posthumus's clothes, thinks the headless Cloten is her beloved Posthumus. This is a variation on a common dramatic device of the time known as the bed trick. We see the bed trick in *All's Well That Ends Well* and *Measure for Measure* too, where overly simple efforts of disguise are extremely effective in very intimate situations.

IS THERE A COMMEDIA INFLUENCE WE CAN CAPITALIZE ON?

The master–servant dynamic is worth utilizing. Cloten is a high-status character, a prince, part of the master class in the Commedia universe, and has a very high opinion of himself that is unwarranted. The ways in which Lord 1 and Lord 2 alternate placating him and making fun of him behind his back is typical Commedia. We see this dynamic at play with Imogen's waiting gentlewoman, Helen, as well. Opportunities for these lower-status members of the nobility to mock Prince Cloten behind his back abound.

There is also textual evidence for a lazzi centering Cloten's odor. It's mentioned twice in the play, but how characters notice and respond to it is unclear. It could be worth developing if you think it would please your audience. Though Cloten is not written in a Capitano archetype, he does have a sword, and he is core to the play's comic relief. It's likely worthwhile to experiment with Capitano-inspired sword lazzi.

CAN WE USE ANY LORD OF MISRULE OR FOOL INFLUENCE?

Cloten is a "natural" fool. His hot-headed and braggart narcissism is a part of him. He is foolish by nature, not by trade. In some ways, he is more unpredictable than we might expect. He alternates between speaking prose and verse. He's incredibly self-centered and emotionally unintelligent, obsessing on trivialities such as Posthumus's clothes while mostly ignoring the obvious: that Imogen does not love him. However, when Cloten speaks for Britain alongside the king and queen in Act

3, he comes across as sincere and committed to a Britain free from Roman rule. In this scene, he is not blatantly foolish, and this behavior combines with his hot-headed narcissism in a nuanced way. We can feel that Cloten is a jerk with serious flaws, but we learn that he's also the kind of person you want on your side in a fight.

Cloten references clothing a great deal. And Helen mentions Cloten's clothes. There could be something in Cloten's everyday costume that distinguishes him visually from the rest of the acting company. His clothes could be trendier or gaudier than those worn by the other characters in the palace. This is in keeping with what was expected from a principal comedian.

WAS CLOTEN WRITTEN FOR KEMP OR ARMIN?

Cloten displays elements of Armin's performance style. He maintains a high-status relationship to the other characters and audience. He sings and is verbally distinct. Cloten is described by Belarius in the middle of the play as having, "snatches in his voice, / And bursts of speaking." We also see Cloten work as part of a trio. It's later in the play when he holds stage alone. Armin's smaller size also increases the chance that Cloten's numerous threats of violence are not seen as credible threats against the play's protagonists. More likely they're perceived by the audience as ridiculous.

CAN WE EMPLOY LESSONS FROM THE CLOWN WORLD?

Yes we can. First, the costume. Cloten is very proud of his clothes, which we can imagine are visually distinct given his wealth and reflect his narcissistic personality and resultant bragging. He's genuinely shocked that Imogen prefers Posthumus's clothes. He mentions clothes regularly throughout the play. When he enters for his last scene in Posthumus's clothes, there is opportunity for a visual gag, especially if the clothes fit Cloten very differently than they fit the romantic lead, Posthumus. It's wise for the actor playing Cloten to develop a relationship with his costume. There's comic opportunity there.

Less obvious but also worth exploring is Cloten's relationship with his sword. He draws his sword at least twice during the play, including in his final scene when he's beheaded offstage. If the practitioner chooses that Cloten's clothes display his wealth and bad sense of fashion, it's plausible that his choice of weaponry would be gaudy as well. If the production goes in that direction, the actor playing Cloten would do well to build a relationship with his weapon using the principles in Chapter 4. Another option would be to simply adopt the Capitano's relationship with his weapon.

Cloten addresses the audience several times during the play, more than is typical with an Armin-based role. He's one of those characters that you wouldn't want as a friend in your everyday life but that you still "love to hate" onstage. He's a stupider version of Iago or Richard III. Cloten's efforts to bond with the audience need to succeed so that they look forward to his return to the stage and expect to laugh when he takes stage.

Also, there's opportunity for signature gestures connected to his endless capacity for threats and insults, particularly in the last scene where his insults and threats culminate with "die the death." This leads to the inevitable, yet hopefully surprising, and perhaps shockingly funny death of Cloten. And then, despite being dead, he keeps getting laughs with his headless corpse. A dream for any comedian.

WHAT ARE THE LANGUAGE OPPORTUNITIES?

There are several language opportunities that stick out, the first one being that Cloten regularly switches between verse and prose. How this informs his character needs to be discovered in rehearsal, but it's a significant clue in the script. At a minimum, when speaking verse, Cloten is more rhythmically controlled than when speaking prose. Throughout both, the use of colons is informative. They often indicate clear places to change focus, clarify the previous phrase, or conduct physical business or short lazzi.

Cloten also speaks a lot of words with sexual connotations. He does this both accidentally and purposefully. His use of F words such as "fit" and "enforced" contain meanings more similar to "fuck." He's intentional with this sexuality when planning to sexually assault Imogen, and discussing his plans to bribe her ladies in waiting is similar to the way one might bribe the servants of chaste Diana. Cloten, however, is likely less intentional when he instructs the musicians he's employed to woo Imogen: "If you can penetrate her with your fingering, so: we'll try with tongue too." Let your desired impact on your audience continue to direct your interpretive choices.

Parting Words

Seven

As mentioned previously, this book wasn't written to cover everything. The lessons shared in this book do not amount to or advocate for a sequential creative process. The uniqueness of each production will dictate if, when, and how to best employ these lessons. However, learning and engaging with the ideas and exercises in this book can provoke new growth in your work on Shakespeare's comedies. Much of this content goes beyond the typical considerations in many conventional rehearsal processes where the practitioners are focused on staging and embodying the script's given circumstances so that the production is clear, cohesive, and entertaining. It takes courage to try new things, and if you decide to start folding these key lessons more fully into your work, I suggest that you give yourself time, communication, and permission to be bold.

If possible, have a couple of conversations or email exchanges between director and actor prior to the start of rehearsals. It can help the actor better understand the director's overall point of view on the play and also get familiar with the intended rehearsal process for accomplishing that vision. It's important that the actor also have an opportunity to express their ideas about their character.

Many actors are afraid of overacting or in other ways appearing unbelievable. This can lead them to hold back with their choices and with their performance. The director should try to embolden the actor early with direction that establishes a vector for purposeful experimentation, one that can have an honest and humorous impact on their audience. It's important for the director to support that boldness and to wield their authority conscientiously. Know that at least some of what the actor creates will not end up in the final product. Deciding what to keep and what to discard is a normal part of any creative process. It's important for the director to ultimately make those calls without shutting down the creative process by coming off as impatient or judgmental. As a director myself, I understand the pressure we can sometimes feel to get the play ready as quickly as possible. We're wise to keep that compulsion in check if we want our actors to genuinely create. As an actor as well, I understand how liberating the freedom to experiment can feel and the richer results that freedom can nurture.

During the process, it's important for the director and all the practitioners to understand what part of the performance is driving the humor. Is it the situation, the physicality, or the language? A comedy will often employ all three to varying degrees, but usually one area will be more important than the others at any given time. I think a fun way to see this in action is in the film *Young Frankenstein*. It can be instructive to notice how the comedic engine of this film trades off between language, visual, and situational humor. Even when all three of these elements appear in a scene, there is usually one that will drive a moment or beat more than the others. It's important to understand this in your production as well so that the practitioners do not unintentionally distract the audience from what is humorous: the words they need to hear, the images they need to see, or the situations they need to appreciate.

Prior to the start of rehearsals, it's helpful if actors begin with Shakespeare's potent language, a core reason why his plays are still enjoyed today. Understand it, speak it, and experiment with it. As you work with the language, take care to remain flexible with your readings and interpretations of the text. The director may have different or additional ideas. The behavior of the other cast members will always necessitate a response that is at least subtly different than what the actor or director initially anticipated. Beware of holding any choice so preciously that change feels impossible. Remain flexible.

Make peace with the fact that each audience will behave at least subtly differently. An important step for any actor seeking to develop rapport with their audience is responding to the behavior of an actual audience. The actor can start getting accustomed to that in rehearsal by responding to the people in the rehearsal room when appropriate. The production will benefit if this actor feels genuinely confident and at ease.

It helps when the production can avoid anxiety, tension, and hurry. Simple directions to the clown or fool, such as "scan the audience when you enter" or "I'd like for you to speak directly to the audience with a soft focus" can be helpful early on. Discussing a preferred status relationship between the clown or fool and the audience can also help the actor rehearse productively. If the director would like the actor to develop signature gestures or other kinds of physical lazzi, let the actor know as soon as possible, encourage their ideas, and give them time to prepare.

I heard an actor refer to their physical comedy process in production as "stocking the fridge": that the actor's job was to fill the metaphorical refrigerator with comedic bits and short lazzi so that the director could then choose ingredients to add to the production. It's a fun way to think about what to include and what to leave out. Just because there are nine kinds of hot sauces in the fridge doesn't mean that all nine have to end up in the soup. The soup tends to turn out better though when the chef has options.

Blocking longer sequences of stage-worthy physical comedy requires more time than selecting from the fridge. Longer lazzi need to remain logical and extremely precise. Though they appear effortless when finished, they take more time to develop and polish than most initially expect. The practitioners must be meticulous with the cause and effect. It's a good idea to schedule some extra time earlier in the process so that all the practitioners can come to an embodied understanding of the style of lazzi the production seeks. When scheduling rehearsals, it can be helpful to think of longer lazzi as similar to how you might think of staged violence or staged intimacy. It takes time for lazzi to grow in a safe, engaging, and repeatable manner.

The director is usually in the best position to discuss costumes and props with the appropriate designers. Onboarding the creative team early can help those departments work productively to facilitate the production's desired impact on its audience. This can be as simple as making sure that the properties designer knows that Pompey will carry Abhorson's chopping block onstage for comedic effect. It can also be clearly communicating with costumes that Cloten's base costume needs to be visually distinct from the others in a wealthy, gaudy way that is both plausible but nevertheless invites the audience to laugh.

***

I wrote this book to inspire and serve twenty-first-century practitioners, educators, scholars, enthusiasts, and students.

If you're an actor or director, I hope that you have new ideas to consider and new questions to ask earlier in your process. I hope these lessons have provoked your creativity in fun and useful ways that more fully capitalize on Shakespeare's comedic dramaturgy: the structure, assumptions, and traditions that influenced his plays. I also hope that I've presented these ideas in ways that can be effectively synthesized with your current process and that can easily pair with your own aesthetic. For all readers, I hope this book helps you more fully engage with the unique challenges and opportunities we find in Shakespeare's comedies.

Shakespeare was an exceptionally effective dramatist who wrote to entertain his audience. He wrote to engage their imaginations. He wrote to have a meaningful, pleasurable, impact on a varied collection of people from a wide range of backgrounds and experiences. When we create productions that do the same for our audiences, we learn from his dramaturgy and honor his intentions. Your audience deserves to experience the joy and humanity in these plays. Shakespeare, comedy, theatre, and all art is for all of us. We want our audiences to feel that way too.

Excerpt from *Applied Meisner for the 21st-Century Actor*

Appendix

CHAPTER 1: WHAT IS ACTING?

It's a simple and often neglected question, maybe because the answer seems obvious. But answering this question and understanding its definition are critical. If we are serious about mastering this craft, we need to know what acting is and what it is not. This will help us focus our training and assess our progress.

When we ask our students "what is acting?" we hear all kinds of answers—it's emotion, it's being realistic, it's "becoming" a character. Haphazard opinions about parts of acting can distract us from committing to what can actually improve your acting. Meisner's definition of acting has an elegant beauty to it. It is simple, easy to remember, and an excellent point of departure.

"Acting is living truthfully under imaginary circumstances."—Sanford Meisner (Meisner and Longwell).

This definition keeps us focused on what is useful because it tells us what acting is and what it is not. Note that the words "performing," "emotion," and "character" are not mentioned. That is because those things are byproducts of living truthfully under imaginary circumstances; they are not our core concerns. We've found that when there is a problem in acting it can always be traced back to the basics. Fully understanding this definition keeps us focused on where to put our attention.

ACTING IS LIVING

What is living? This simple question is the subject of numerous books but for actors it is most useful to understand living as experiencing the continuous push and pull of individual moments. Meisner called this the pinch and the ouch (Meisner and Longwell 35). That is, you experience behavior from another person (the pinch) and then respond with behavior of your own (the ouch). This is the pulse of living and it is continually present in our everyday lives.

Real life is fluid and alive. Your acting should be too. Life is full of pinch–ouch or the cause to effect reality. That is what we mean by "living."

PINCH–OUCH

Cause to effect reality is how most people see and interpret their world. Something happens that then causes another thing to happen. You feel a pinch and then you ouch. When acting, the pinch must be experienced before the ouch can happen. When a pinch–ouch is happening between actors the audience views the acting as truthful. It is the give-and-take of an alive event. When actors "ouch" without having experienced a "pinch" the moment will not appear truthful because the "ouch" is not justified without first feeling a pinch. Listening for pinches, and then responding with ouches is the fluid moment-to-moment life necessary for truthful acting.

There are other terms that describe the pinch–ouch reality: cause–effect, action–reaction, tickle–laugh (also Meisner) and trigger–heap are some commonly used terms. Pinch–ouch however reminds us to train viscerally. The cause-to-effect, moment-to-moment reality should be physically experienced similar to how you physically experience an actual pinch.

ACTING IS LIVING TRUTHFULLY

Acting is living truthfully as opposed to lying, which also includes omitting parts of the truth. In everyday life you may view withholding certain parts of your truth as necessary or even helpful to your situation and that's your choice. Know that most people do not live their complete personal truth in everyday life. When asked, "How are you?" you may often respond with the socially acceptable answer, "good," even though you are having a terrible day. If they get your order wrong at a restaurant, you may be polite to the server while inwardly fuming. These are times when you withhold your truth and society deems it acceptable and even "correct." When acting, withholding any part of your personal, subjective truth in the moment is not useful. Commit to living truthfully within the imaginary world.

Note that there is no mention in this definition of "naturally," "realistically," or "believably." We have observed that when students are consciously or unconsciously trying to accomplish those things their acting becomes flaccid and ordinary—at times almost apologetic. Words like "realistically" tend to dull our authentic edge. Focus on telling the truth, your authentic truth in the moment, and trust that those other things will take care of themselves.

Don't confuse truthful with being necessarily dangerous or reckless. That's not part of the definition of acting either. Respect boundaries.

ACTING IS LIVING TRUTHFULLY UNDER

Why the word "under"? Why not the word "in"? They're easy to interchange in Meisner's definition but we've come to appreciate "under" because it implies the pressure that a story's imaginary circumstances put on you.

"Plays are Written About the Day Something Happens"—Brant Pope

We regularly heard this phrase from our teachers while training, and it applies to all good stories. Scripts are written about the day a critical event (or crisis) occurs in a life: life, death, love, betrayal, etc. These crises are not necessarily unpleasant, but they are intense and typically rare in one's everyday life. They are the moments when our dreams or nightmares are about to unfold, are unfolding, or have just happened. As actors we get to live truthfully under this kind of heightened, story-worthy, make-believe.

Some examples of the day that something special happens:

- In the classical Greek drama *Oedipus Rex*, Oedipus is the King of Thebes during a plague and all goes wrong in his kingdom.
- In Lorraine Hansberry's *Raisin in the Sun*, Walter works to purchase a home within a racist and segregated society, not a progressive one.
- In Henrik Ibsen's *Hedda Gabler*, Hedda seeks liberation within a sexist marriage rather than one built on equality.

ACTING IS LIVING TRUTHFULLY UNDER IMAGINARY CIRCUMSTANCES

The writer has created the script's Imaginary Circumstances or the premise of the story (things like the characters, the conflict, the dialogue), but they cannot provide everything. As actors it is our job to read between the lines and imagine additional, useful, circumstances that help us justify and fully commit to the imaginary situation. These fully realized circumstances are then brought to life in our acting. We call this crafting, and you will learn to effectively craft as you work through this book.

CRAFT TO CARE

How you chose to work with Imaginary Circumstances is very important. The choice is simple: you either choose to make choices that help you care more or help you care less. "Craft to care" is a mantra we use in our teaching. Engage with the imaginary circumstances and craft your choices so that you can more fully care and commit to the make-believe situation.

A predicament of our 21st century reality is that we are regularly confronted by terrible, sometimes nightmarish events occurring globally and locally. While being aware is part of good citizenship, over time this continuous onslaught of bad news can cause a kind of emotional callousing where we unintentionally cope by learning to care less. You may find yourself thinking: "After all, despite the latest disaster, my kids still need me to take them to practice." This is an understandable habit for coping with the downside of life, but that habit is not useful when acting. "Craft to care." Understand the writer's imaginary circumstances and flesh them out with your imagination to help you care more and fully commit to the situation.

Bibliography

Barber, Cesar Lombardi. *Shakespeare's Festive Comedy: A Study of Dramatic Form and Its Relation to Social Custom.* Princeton, NJ: Princeton University Press, 1959.

Barton, John. *Playing Shakespeare: An Actor's Guide.* London: Methuen, 1984.

Basil, John with Gunning, Stephanie. *Will Power: How to Act Shakespeare in 21 Days.* New York: Applause Theatre & Cinema Books, 2006.

Berry, Cicely. *The Actor and the Text.* New York: Applause, 2000.

Boleslavsky, Richard. *Acting, the First Six Lessons.* New York: Theatre Arts Inc., 1969.

Bruder, Melissa, Cohn, Lee Michael, Olenek, Madeline, Pollack, Nathaniel, Previto, Robert, Zigler, Scott, and Mamet, David. *A Practical Handbook for the Actor.* New York: Vintage Books, 1986.

Callery, Dymphna. *Through the Body: A Practical Guide to Physical Theatre.* London and New York: Routledge and Nick Hern Books, 2001.

Davison, Jon. *Clown.* New York: Palgrave Macmillan, 2013.

Duchartre, Pierre-Louis. *The Italian Comedy: The Improvisation, Scenarios, Lives, Portraits, and Masks of the Illustrious Characters of the Commedia dell'arte.* New York: Dover, 1966.

Fava, Antonio. *The Comic Mask in the Commedia dell'arte: Actor Training, Improvisation, and the Poetics of Survival.* Evanston, IL: Northwestern University Press, 2007.

Grantham, Barry. *Playing Commedia: A Training Guide to Commedia Techniques*. Portsmouth, NH: Heinemann, 2000.

Johnstone, Keith. *Impro: Improvisation and the Theatre*. New York: Theatre Arts Books, 1979.

Kissel, Howard. *Stella Adler: The Art of Acting*. New York; London: Applause, 2001.

Lecoq, Jacques with Carasso, Jean-Gabriel and Lallias, Jean-Claude. *The Moving Body: Teaching Creative Theatre*. London and New York: Routledge, 2000.

Meagher, John C. *Shakespeare's Shakespeare: How the Plays Were Made*. New York: Continuum, 1997.

Meisner, Sanford and Longwell, Dennis. *Sanford Meisner on Acting*. New York: Vintage, 1987.

Otos, Kevin and Shively, Kim. *Applied Meisner for the 21st-Century Actor*. London and New York: Routledge, 2021.

Robinson, Davis Rider. *The Physical Comedy Handbook*. Portsmouth: Heinemann, 1999.

Rodenburg, Patsy. *Speaking Shakespeare: Voice and the Performer*. Basingstoke and New York: Palgrave Macmillan, 2002.

Rudlin, John. *Commedia dell'arte: An Actor's Handbook*. London and New York: Routledge, 1994.

Schechter, Joel. *The Pickle Clowns: New American Circus Comedy*. Carbondale and Edwardsville, IL: Southern Illinois University Press, 2001.

Simon, Eli. *The Art of Clowning*. Basingstoke and New York: Palgrave Macmillan, 2009.

Videbaek, Bente A. *The Stage Clown in Shakespeare's Theatre*. Westport, CT: Greenwood Press, 1996.

Weimann, Robert. *Shakespeare and the Popular Tradition in the Theatre: Studies in the Social Dimension of Dramatic Form and Function*. Baltimore, MD: Johns Hopkins University Press, 1978.

Wiles, David. *Shakespeare's Clown: Actor and Text in Shakespeare's Playhouse*. Cambridge: Press Syndicate of the University of Cambridge, 1987.

Printed in the United States
by Baker & Taylor Publisher Services